GREAT SPORTS HOAXES

george sullivan

SCHOLASTIC INC.
New York Toronto London Auckland Sydney Tokyo

ISBN 0–590–32181–1

Copyright © 1983 by George Sullivan. All rights reserved. Published by Scholastic Inc.

12 11 10 9 8 7 6 5 4 3 2 1   12   3 4 5 6 7/8

Printed in the U. S. A.   06

Introduction

Early one October morning in 1978, Captain Thomas Burton of the New York City Police Department was on his way to work, when he noticed something strange. Two men and a woman were busily painting a blue line down the center of Vernon Boulevard in Long Island City.

Captain Burton watched the trio for a few minutes, then suddenly realized what was afoot. The New York City Marathon, with many thousands of runners weaving through the streets of the city's five boroughs, was scheduled for the next day. Marathon officials had painted a wide blue line on the streets to guide the runners.

The painters that Captain Burton was watching were putting down a fake line, one that would mean an unplanned detour for the contestants. If the runners were to follow it, they would end up on the back streets of the borough of Queens. The official line directed the runners to make a right turn across the Queensboro Bridge into Manhattan.

Captain Burton arrested the three painters. They were charged with criminal mischief and tampering with a traffic control device.

"Why did they do it?" Captain Burton was asked.

"Just for kicks, I guess," he answered.

There are many kinds of hoaxes, but the one

1

described above, which takes the form of a practical joke, is undoubtedly the most common.

But there are others that have no humor to them. These are hoaxes that are meant not only to deceive but to defraud. A fast racehorse will be substituted for a slow one. A basketball player will attempt to "shave" points in a game. In either case, a betting swindle is the object.

Hoaxes are almost as common to sports as glittering trophies and sore muscles. Indeed, it would take a book several times the size of this one to set down all the stories of sports hoaxers and their exploits. The most notable of them are recounted here.

Contents

1

The Great Pretender

One winter afternoon early in 1979, Barry Bremen, a thirty-two-year-old life insurance salesman who loved sports, was playing basketball with some friends at the Jewish Community Center in the Detroit suburb of West Bloomfield. Someone mentioned the forthcoming National Basketball Association All-Star Game. It was to be played in a few weeks just down the road at the Silverdome, a new arena in Pontiac, Michigan. All of the best professional players would be there.

"I bet I could go out there with those guys and make a few baskets," Bremen said with a grin.

"I'll bet you couldn't," said one of his friends.

One word led to another. A wager was made. Barry Bremen had to sneak onto the court at the nationally televised game and put a basket through the hoop. If he did that, he would be richer by three hundred dollars.

Bremen plotted carefully. He acquired an old Kansas City Kings warm-up uniform. The jacket had once belonged to Ollie Johnson and the pants to Bill Robinzine, both former members of the Kansas City team.

Bremen wore the uniform as he watched the first half of the game from a darkened runway leading to the court. When the two teams filed back into the arena for the second half, the six-foot-one Bremen made his move, slipping into the line of players that made up the West team.

The team began its warm-up drills, with the players shooting practice baskets. Bremen joined in. Jack Sikma of the Seattle SuperSonics looked at him quizzically. "Stay cool, fellas," Bremen pleaded. "I need to make a basket. I've got a bet going." Sikma shrugged. Neither he or any of the other players seemed to mind.

Someone fed Bremen the ball. He dribbled in for a lay-up, but he was so nervous that he missed the basket entirely. He missed his shot a second and third time. Finally, taking a pass from George McGinnis of the Denver Nuggets, Bremen banked the ball off the backboard and into the net.

Bremen wore a wide smile as he hurried off the court. He had earned three hundred dollars for only a few minutes work.

That might have been the end of it, except that photographers at courtside noticed what had happened. The next day, photos of Bremen frolicking amidst the best basketball players in America appeared in newspapers from coast-to-coast. A producer from NBC Television's *Today* show saw one of the photos and called Bremen, inviting him to come to New York to be interviewed by Dick Schaap.

Bremen had crashed the big time. His career was launched.

In the months that followed, Bremen played nine holes of golf during a practice round at the U.S. Open, the outstanding golf event of the year. He shagged flies in the outfield before baseball's All-Star Game. He roamed the sidelines as an All Star at the National Football League's All-Star Game in the disguise of a referee.

Bremen's fame grew by leaps and bounds. Besides being a guest on the *Today* show, he appeared on the *Tonight Show* with Johnny Carson. He dined at the exclusive Polo Lounge in Los Angeles and hobnobbed with the celebrities at the famous Studio 54 in New York. He was featured in *People* and other national magazines.

"I can't believe what's happened," he said. "I've gotten so much publicity, it's unbelievable. Everywhere I go, people keep asking me, 'What are you going to do next?'

"It has been like a dream come true. I always wanted to be an athlete. Now I'm living out my dream."

Bremen's dreams would never have been realized were it not for the cooperation he received from certain athletes. At the All-Star baseball game at the Kingdome in Seattle in 1979, Bremen showed up in a tailor-made Yankee uniform, which he wore beneath his street clothes. Using a phony press pass, he gained admittance to the field before the game. He made his way to the American League dugout where he met Kansas City third baseman George Brett. Bremen told Brett exactly what he planned to do. Brett grinned, then escorted Barry past security guards into the American League locker room. Once they had arrived there, Brett said, "Okay, do your Superman change."

After Bremen had stripped off his street clothes, he trotted out onto the field. He chased down fly balls for a while and chatted with the players.

"I'm Barry Bremen," he said, shaking hands with Sid Monge, a relief pitcher for the Cleveland Indians. "I'm an impostor."

"I'm an impostor, too," said Monge with a straight face.

Not long before the game was to begin, Bremen was asked to swap uniforms with Reggie Jackson, the Yankee superstar. Jackson's equipment had not arrived. So Barry gave Reggie his homemade Yankee uniform in exchange for a Seattle Mariner uniform that Jackson had borrowed earlier.

Game time was drawing near. Barry lined up in the dugout with the other American League stars. One by one they were introduced to the fans in the stadium and the television cameras. An official from the TV network presenting the game kept scanning the line. He was aware that Bruce Bochte, an infielder, was the only member of the Seattle team on the All-Star squad. When the official saw Barry in his Mariner uniform, he knew immediately that something was wrong. He quickly yanked Bremen out of the line.

Bremen was a fine amateur golfer, so it was only natural that he would choose the U.S. Open Tournament as a scene for another of his charades. The Open was played at the Inverness Club in Toledo that year. After Kip Byrne and

Wayne Levi, two professional players, had finished the first nine holes of their eighteen-hole practice round, Barry asked whether he could join them for the second nine holes. He explained he was an amateur playing in his first U.S. Open. "We're glad to have you play along," Levi said.

Barry had only one anxious moment during the time he spent on the hallowed Inverness course. He hooked one of his drives into the crowd lining the fairway. "My God!" he thought to himself. "What if I've hit somebody. People will start asking questions and find out who I am." But the incident passed without causing Barry any difficulty.

On the eighteenth hole, Barry experienced one of the biggest thrills of his "career." His approach shot to the green landed in a sand trap. When it was his turn to hit, Barry went down into the trap, adjusted his feet in the sand, then whipped the clubhead into the ball with a smooth and rhythmic swing. The ball popped high into the air and came down within three feet of the cup, where it stopped dead. Hundreds of fans had ringed the green and, when they saw Barry's splendid effort, cheered him loudly. Barry took off his cap and waved it. "It was a moment every golfer dreams of," he said afterward.

Barry's appearance at the National Football League's Pro Bowl in Honolulu in January 1980 was less of a triumph for him. Again he used bogus press credentials to gain entry to the field. Over a football uniform that had once belonged to Lem Barney, a cornerback for the Detroit Lions who had retired two years before, Barry

7

wore slacks, a turtleneck sweater, and a wool sports jacket.

He paced the sidelines as he waited for the teams to come out onto the field so he could spring his surprise. The day was hot and humid. Beads of perspiration rolled down his forehead. His black hair began to curl. He sat down on one of the team benches and mopped his face with a handkerchief.

A number of fans, noticing his plight, began to jeer at him. "Hey, you jerk," said one, "why don't you take off your coat?"

A photographer who was readying his equipment in anticipation of the players' arrival asked Barry the same question. Barry fumbled for an answer, finally explaining that he suffered from a skin disease and had to protect himself from the sun.

The longer he waited, the more conspicuous he felt. The stadium was filling up, and Barry kept imagining that every pair of eyes was focused on him as he sat and sweated. Finally, the players began to trickle out onto the field, first the kickers and the punt returners, the quarterbacks and pass receivers, and, eventually, the other members of both squads. Barry breathed a sigh of relief as he slipped off his outer clothing.

For the next few minutes, Barry enjoyed himself posing as Lem Barney. He did some light jogging and performed a few stretching exercises, mixing in with the other defensive players on the National Football Conference team. These included Roger Wehrli of the St. Louis Cardinals, Lemar Parrish of the Washington Redskins, and

Tom Myers of the New Orleans Saints. If any of these players was aware of Bremen's ruse, he kept the knowledge to himself.

The equipment manager of the National Football Conference squad was the first to realize that Barry was an impostor. He became suspicious when he took notice of the skin color of the player with the name "Barney" blazoned across his shoulders. Lem Barney was black. The person inside Barney's uniform was not. The equipment manager pointed this out to an official. Within minutes, Barry was being led out of Aloha Stadium, even though Roger Wehrli and other players kept insisting to the officials that they were making a mistake, that Bremen was really Barney.

Barry's next scheme was even more of a failure. It involved the National Hockey League's All-Star Game, held at Joe Louis Arena in Detroit. This time, instead of posing as a player, Barry decided to play the role of an official. It was no trouble obtaining skates, dark trousers, and an official's striped shirt.

Not long before the game was to begin, Barry trailed along behind the three authentic officials as they made their way to the rink. However, a delay during the introductions caused them to be halted at the edge of the ice.

Linesman John D'Amico noticed the stranger in the black-and-white striped shirt. "Who are you?" he said, his face twisting into a scowl. "What are you doing here?"

Barry had a ready answer. "I'm the alternate judge," he replied. "I'm here to check the nets."

"Check the what?" said D'Amico.

9

Then D'Amico spotted the NHL emblem that Barry had pinned to the front of his striped shirt. He hadn't been able to obtain a woven emblem so had cut one from the side of a cardboard box.

"A cardboard emblem?" said D'Amico. "That's pretty shabby, isn't it?"

Security guards were summoned and Barry was led from the arena. It was all very routine for him now. He was brought to a police room beneath the arena, where a report was filled out. But he was not arrested or treated as a lawbreaker. Instead, a photographer was brought in and several of the police officers had their pictures taken with Barry, and many asked for his autograph.

Only once in his role as The Great Pretender did Barry run into real difficulty. One of his dreams was to pass as a Dallas Cowboys' cheerleader. He sought to make the dream a reality during a Dallas Cowboys-Washington Redskins game at Texas Stadium.

He prepared for the hoax by shaving his legs and having a duplicate of the cheerleader uniform custom-made. The caper cost him one thousand two hundred dollars of his own money.

Once the game was underway, Bremen burst onto the sidelines. He wore white vinyl boots, hot pants, a blonde wig, and a halter top over a padded bra.

He got out only one "Go, Dallas!" before security guards hauled him off the field, ripping off his wig and handcuffing him.

Always in the past, Bremen's targets had laughed at his antics. Not the Cowboys. They charged him with trespassing and creating a nuisance, and sued him for five thousand dollars. They also barred him from attending any future games of the Cowboys.

Bremen's six-year-old son, Noah, the oldest of his three children, was upset by the ban. The Cowboys happened to be his favorite team.

Bremen himself does not have happy memories of the hoax. "It was tough shaving my legs and dressing up like a woman," he said. "I wouldn't go through that again."

His wife Margo once sought to explain his mischief by saying that Barry is "fulfilling a grand fantasy to be in the limelight." To other prospective impostors who seek to imitate his feats, Barry has this advice: "Don't do it. It's against the law. Stay away. This is *my* act."

2

Olympic Trickery

The Olympic Games have a rich and colorful history. They were originated by the ancient Greeks more than two thousand years ago, and held regularly until the year 392 A.D.

In 1896, after a lapse of more than fifteen hundred years, the Olympics were revived. They have been staged every four years since, except for interruptions caused by World War I and World War II.

Sports competition has been only one feature of the Olympics. What's happening in the stadium can be overshadowed by controversy, confusion, bickering, or injustice.

There have been hoaxes, too.

Some hoaxers are attracted by the worldwide audience the Olympics attract. They realize that if they are successful their deed will be long remembered.

Russia's Boris Onischenko, a contestant in the 1976 Olympics at Montreal, had the more usual reason. He tried to perpetrate a hoax to win a gold medal.

Onischenko had come close to being a gold medalist in the 1972 Olympic Games, when he won the silver medal for the Soviet Union in the event in which he specialized, the modern pentathlon. This is a five-event contest which consists of pistol shooting, a three hundred-meter swim, a four thousand-meter cross country race, a five thousand-meter steeplechase on an unfamiliar horse, and épée fencing.

Onischenko's attempt at hoaxing concerned the épée, a fencing sword with a stiff, three-sided blade that tapers to a blunted point. In competition, a contestant scores a hit when he manages to reach the target — any part of his opponent's body — with the tip of his épée. It is a difficult and demanding form of competition.

In the Olympic Games, as in all major épée competitions, an electronic scoring system is used. The épée has an electrical contact mounted within its tip. The contact is connected by a wire that runs through the hollow blade, up the fencer's sword arm, and around his back to a signaling device at the scorer's table. All hits by either fencer are thus immediately recorded.

Before the épée competition began in the 1976 Olympics, Onischenko tampered with his sword. He installed special wiring and a button in the épée handle. When the button was pressed, it caused a signal that registered as a hit at the scorer's table. In theory, at least, Onischenko could have won any of his matches merely by sitting in the locker room and pressing the button.

Onischenko's hoax might have been successful but, as an English poet once noted, "There is no armor against fate." Onischenko's opponent was Jeremy Fox of England. The match had hardly begun when Onischenko lunged at Fox, flicking his sword toward the Englishman's chest. Fox jumped back without being touched. But at the scorer's table and on the scoreboard high above the competitors, green and red lights flashed and a buzzer sounded, crediting Onischenko with a hit.

Fox gasped in astonishment. Onischenko's blade had missed him by a mile. He started protesting loudly.

Officials quickly ringed the two men. One of the officials asked whether he might inspect Onischenko's épée. The Russian had no choice but to hand it over. The button in the handle was quickly discovered. The judges realized that Onischenko had tried to fool them.

Onischenko claimed the épée was not his personal property. But the officials refused to accept this explanation. The day following the incident, Onischenko was ordered to fly back to the Soviet Union.

"What an idiot!" said an official of the Modern Pentathlon Union. It was generally agreed that Onischenko had no need to rig his épée. He probably would have won without resorting to such deception.

Onischenko was not greeted warmly when he returned to the Soviet Union. He was ousted from the various athletic clubs to which he belonged. In Kiev, where he lived and worked as a teacher at the Dynamo Sports Institute, he was reduced to a job as an assistant director of one of the city's municipal swimming pools. Seldom has Olympic trickery been so costly.

The Olympic marathon has been the target of hoaxers at least twice, most recently in 1972. The Olympics were held in Munich, Germany, that year.

As a marathon got underway, America's Frank Shorter sprinted into the lead. As he sped through the twisting streets of the city, he kept lengthening his lead. By the halfway point, no one was close to him. He kept pushing and pushing. "My God!" he said to himself as he neared the Munich Sports Stadium and the finish line, "I've really done it!"

Inside the stadium, tens of thousands of spectators sat spellbound awaiting Shorter's arrival. Every eye was focused on the tunnel at one end of the stadium that linked the stadium track with the street outside.

When a lean and fragile figure in a blue and orange track outfit emerged from the tunnel and began to circle the track, the crowd let out a thunderous roar. As the runner made his way around the track, the crowd stood and cheered.

Erich Segal, a well-known author and runner, a broadcaster for *ABC's Wide World of Sports* that afternoon, was the first to realize what was afoot.

"That's not Frank! That's not Frank!" Segal screamed into his microphone.

"The guy is an imposter," Segal continued. "That used to happen in the Boston Marathon. That guy is an imposter. Get him off the track."

The phony marathoner was approaching the finish line when Shorter came out of the tunnel and began circling the track. The crowd, thinking that he was the runner-up, welcomed him with polite applause. Shorter's face wore a confused look. He had expected he would be greeted with more enthusiasm. His heart sank. "Someone must have finished ahead of me," he thought.

Shorter turned to see Erich Segal running at his side. Still clutching his microphone, Segal shouted, "You won, Frank! You won! The other guy is an imposter." Shorter grinned in relief.

Following the finish, the imposter identified himself as a European college student. He said he had hidden inside the tunnel leading to the Stadium. When he spotted Shorter approaching, he raced through the tunnel and onto the stadium track.

Why did he do it? It was in the cause of peace, he said. He had worn a T-shirt bearing the picture of a dove.

A hoax attempt in the 1904 Olympic marathon was of a more serious nature. St. Louis played host to the games that year. Since only a few foreign countries sent teams to St. Louis, 1904 being a time long before the dawn of commercial air travel, the games that year had a distinctly American flavor. Of the seventy-five medals awarded in track and field, for instance, seventy went to American athletes. In boxing and wrestling, there were no foreign contestants at all.

The marathon was a 25-mile race in those days. Not until 1908, when the Olympic Games were held in London, would the race distance be standardized at 26 miles, 385 yards. For the 1904 Olympics, the competition began in the stadium, with the contestants running about 12.5 miles out into the country, and then 12.5 miles back.

There were thirty-one entries. Seventeen represented the United States, ten were from Greece, three from South Africa, and one from Cuba.

As a group, the runners bore only a slight resemblance to the well-trained, highly experienced athletes who have competed in recent Olympic marathons. Two of the South African entrants were runners in name only. They worked at concession stands at the St. Louis Exposition grounds, and entered the race more on a whimsical impulse than anything else.

Pint-sized Felix Carvajal, the Cuban, was a postman in his native Havana. To raise money to finance his trip to St. Louis, he would run around the great public square in Havana until a crowd gathered. Then he would hop up on a wooden box and beg for contributions to enable him to get to St. Louis.

Marathon day was broiling hot, the kind of day that can be typical in St. Louis in the summer. Dozens of chugging autos, primitive and strange-looking by today's standards, were on hand to carry officials, handlers, coaches, and medical personnel along the route.

Felix Carvajal came up to the starting line wearing a long sleeved shirt and long trousers. Someone took pity on him and, with a heavy scissors, snipped off the sleeves of his shirt and cut his trousers so they somewhat resembled running shorts.

As the starter raised his pistol and the runners

toed the line, a squad of horsemen dashed down the roadway to clear the course of spectators. At the gun, the Cuban went to the front and stayed there. Other runners were soon dropping out because of the heat and the clouds of choking dust raised by the automobiles. Neither of these seemed to bother Felix. He laughed and cracked jokes with the spectators and picked apples and ate them along the way. But eventually the blistering heat took its toll, and Felix dropped out of the lead. He would finish fifth.

As the runners passed the halfway mark and headed back to the stadium, it was apparent that the winner would be one of a handful of Americans. Sam Mellon of New York was in the lead as the runners headed home, but he was soon overtaken by Thomas Hicks of Cambridge, Massachusetts.

Hicks was a pitiful figure. His handlers kept sponging him off with warm water and gave him sips of stimulants to keep him going. He seemed to be running in a trance, never speaking, never acknowledging the assistance of his handlers.

Of the thirty-one runners who started, only fourteen would finish. Fred Lorz of the Mohawk (New York) Athletic Club was one of the starters. After he covered about nine miles, Lorz was seized with severe leg cramps. The pain kept getting worse. Lorz finally gave up all thought of finishing the race and accepted a ride from a passing auto. He continued toward the stadium in comfort, waving at the others, shouting words of encouragement to them as he passed them by.

After ten or eleven miles, the auto in which

Lorz was riding broke down, a common occurrence in the case of vehicles of the day. Lorz had to get to the stadium because his clothes were there, so he started jogging. The time he spent in the automobile had refreshed him, and he made quick work of the four or five miles he had to cover.

In the stadium, the crowd waited feverishly in the hot sun. The runners were well behind schedule, which added to the crowd's impatience.

Fred Lorz was the first runner to enter the stadium. He was jogging easily, grinning from ear to ear, hardly a speck of dust on him. When the crowd sighted Lorz, they exploded.

A bewildered look crossed Lorz's face. Then, as officials surrounded him, shaking his hands, clapping him on the back, Lorz realized he was being mistaken as the winner. But he didn't say anything. He was carried about in triumph and photographed with Alice Roosevelt, the daughter of President Theodore Roosevelt.

Looking back, most Olympic historians agree that Lorz was merely playing a joke on the judges and other officials. He knew that other runners and the race officials out on the course were fully aware that he had dropped out of the race. He kept his secret to himself, however, and allowed events to take their course.

If a joke was Lorz's intention, the joke suddenly backfired. About fifteen minutes after Lorz's arrival, the glassy-eyed Hicks came stumbling into the stadium, handlers at each side of him, ready to catch him should he fall. Told that Hicks had finished second, the officials who had followed the race in cars rushed at Lorz, calling him a crook, a cheat, a snake, and several other names. In a matter of minutes, Hicks was named the rightful winner.

It didn't make much of a difference to Hicks who won the race. Without even receiving his medal, he was placed on a stretcher and carried to the dressing room where several doctors worked over him, simply getting him in condition to leave the grounds. He missed the awards ceremony and his gold medal had to be given to him several days later.

Hicks' time of three hours, twenty-eight minutes, fifty-three seconds, for the race is probably the best evidence of the ghastly conditions that prevailed. In the two previous Olympics, the winning time had been less than three hours. Modern-day running champions are able to speed over the marathon course, longer by more than a mile than the distance Hicks ran, in not much more than two hours.

As for Fred Lorz, his story that he was only trying to play a joke was eventually believed. He was allowed to compete again and became the United States marathon champion in 1905.

One of the strangest of all Olympics hoaxes concerned the famous Press sisters, Tamara and Irina, who represented the Soviet Union.

Tamara, who was big for a woman, weighing over two hundred pounds, and heavily muscled, was better known than her sister. In the 1960 Olympics in Rome, she set a record in the shot put, hurling the eight-pound, thirteen-ounce iron ball a distance of 56 feet, 9⅞ inches. That was two feet farther than any female competitor had ever thrown the shot before.

In 1964, when the Games were held in Tokyo, Tamara was even more remarkable, beating her Olympic record with a throw of 59 feet, 6 inches.

That same year, Tamara also won the discus with a throw of 187 feet, 10 inches, eclipsing the previous record by more than 7 feet. Irina Press won the women's pentathlon competition in 1964.

But there were rumors about the Press sisters. It was whispered that they were men, not women.

Olga Fikatova Connolly, who won a gold medal in the discus at the 1956 Olympics, and who now lives in Los Angeles, was a friend of the Press sisters. "Tamara would never undress in the presence of other girls," Connolly once recalled. "She would always shower separately."

"She was a very sad, awkward person. I felt sorry for her. I once told her, 'Why don't you make yourself pretty?' I took her to a beauty shop. But she was so uncomfortable she went back to her room and braided her hair in two braids again."

The story of the Press sisters came to an abrupt end. To still the rumors surrounding them and other female athletes, officials representing the international sports community began asking athletes to take sex tests. The tests were first used in the 1967 European Cup track and field championships. Once the tests began, Tamara and Irina Press disappeared from international sports competition, never to be heard from again.

3

Rosie

When tall, dark-haired, twenty-six-year-old Rosie Ruiz came pounding down Boylston Street in the final half-mile of the 1980 Boston Marathon, spectators lining the roadway screamed in delight. Not only was she streaking to victory over the 448 other women in the race, but she was winging along at a record pace. She crossed the finish line in the time of two hours, thirty-one minutes, fifty-six seconds, slumping into the arms of officials. No woman had ever run the Boston Marathon faster.

When she was told she had just won, a look of surprise crossed her face. Then a victory wreath was placed upon her head. Ruiz smiled proudly and waved both arms to the cheering crowd.

But from the instant she crossed the finish line, questions about Ruiz and her performance began to be asked. Ruiz did not look like someone who had just run twenty-six-plus miles. Her hair was not matted with perspiration, even though the day was blistering hot. Ruiz wasn't even panting at the finish.

And then there was Ruiz herself, her appearance. Several runners noticed that she wasn't particularly fit looking. She had the beginnings of a double chin. She had flabby thighs. Marathon runners do not have double chins or flabby thighs. They are greyhound-sleek from head to toe.

Did Rosie Ruiz *really* win the Boston Marathon in 1980? Or was she an imposter, someone who played the role of champion, finishing a race she didn't even start by slipping into the competition at a point not far from the finish line?

All available evidence points to the latter.

To weigh the evidence, it's important to first understand the character of a marathon. It is one of the most punishing of all sports events, a foot-race that covers 26 miles, 385 yards, over public roads closed to traffic.

Merely to enter a marathon and finish is a remarkable feat. It is an ordeal that compares to swimming the English Channel or climbing Mt. Everest. It is three hours of steadily increasing pain and self doubt, a struggle not to quit, not to falter, to surmount that next hill, to get around that next turn, to run just one more mile and, toward the end, just one more step.

Up until fairly recent times, women weren't permitted to run in most marathons. They were considered too delicate for the grueling test. That feeling began to change in the late 1960s. During the next decade, the barriers started coming down. Women were first permitted to run in the Boston Marathon in 1972.

The Boston Marathon is the oldest American marathon of them all, dating to 1897. It is also one of the biggest, drawing more than four thousand entries and about half-a-million spectators each year. The spectators line the course from the starting point in Hopkinton to the finish line at the Prudential Center in downtown Boston, standing ten and twelve deep in some places.

The men and women who are capable of doing well in marathon competition are a tightly-knit group. Not only do they compete together throughout the year, they often train together. They all know one another. But not one of the other marathoners knew Rosie Ruiz; none had ever heard of her. She was a mystery woman.

After the race, when reporters started asking Ruiz questions, more doubts were raised. Ruiz told the reporters she had been born in Cuba, came to Miami with her mother and other relatives when she was seven, had graduated from Wayne State University in Detroit, and currently lived in New York City where she did clerical work for a company that dealt in stocks and bonds. Ruiz told the reporters that the Boston race was the second marathon in which she had competed. She said she had run the New York City Marathon in the fall of 1979, finishing with a time of two hours, fifty-six minutes, twenty-nine seconds.

"How much training do you do?" a reporter asked.

"About sixty-five miles a week," said Ruiz.

"Do you run intervals?" another reporter asked. (An interval is a training technique which involves alternately running fast and jogging over a set distance.)

Ruiz frowned. "What's an interval?" she said.

"What was your ten-mile split?" still another

reporter asked. (A split is a runner's time over a measured distance.)

"What's a split?" said Ruiz.

The reporters could hardly believe their ears. It seemed incredible that the woman just crowned champion of the Boston Marathon didn't know two common terms that runners use.

But Ruiz would not allow herself to be shaken by the questions. "I don't know how to explain what I did," she said. "I just got up this morning with a lot of energy."

In the days that followed, evidence mounted that Ruiz was guilty of cheating.

Susan Morrow, a New York photographer, told of meeting Ruiz, who was dressed in running clothes and wearing a race number, on a subway on the day of the New York City Marathon. Ruiz explained to Morrow that she had started the race but dropped out because she had sprained her ankle.

The two women rode the subway to a stop near Central Park. Together they walked to the finish line.

Ruiz wandered into the area where the runners gathered. She asked officials to treat her injured ankle, and she was whisked away to the medical area.

Then another witness came forward, Cindy Wuss, a runner from Brooklyn. Wuss had run the New York City Marathon in the time of two hours, fifty-six minutes, twenty-seven seconds, two seconds ahead of the time with which Ruiz had been credited.

Wuss explained that she had finished strongly,

seeking to pass other women so she could improve her place in standings. As she swept toward the finish line, Wuss recalled passing and seeing only one other woman, Marilyn Bevans of Baltimore. Rosie was nowhere to be seen.

When officials screened videotape of the finish, what they saw supported Wuss's description of the finish. They saw Wuss finish, then two men, then Marilyn Bevans, then another man, but no other woman for another four seconds.

If Rosie Ruiz did not actually cross the finish line, how was she credited with an official time of two hours, fifty-six minutes, twenty-nine seconds?

One official figured it out. On his or her number, each runner wears a small coded symbol that is removed and read electronically when he or she crosses the finish line. When Ruiz was taken to the medical area for treatment to her ankle, her coded tag was taken from her number by a messenger and fed into the electronic scanner.

A few days later, Fred Lebow, the director of the New York City Marathon, disqualified Ruiz's finish in that event. "Rosie did not finish the race," he declared.

Meanwhile, officials of the Boston Marathon were conducting an investigation of their own. They interviewed their race spotters, individuals stationed along the route at various points who check the performances of the leading runners. None of the checkers reported seeing Rosie.

And none of the hundreds of reporters covering the race could recall seeing her, either — except at the finish line. Ruiz did not appear in even one of the more than ten thousand photographs taken during the race.

Perhaps the most damaging evidence was offered by two race spectators, both Harvard students. They told reporters that they had seen a woman jump into the race at about a half mile from the finish line. The incident occurred at the time Ruiz would have passed that point to cross the finish line when she did.

So it was that one week to the day after she had received the victor's laurels in Boston, Ruiz was disqualified. Jacqueline Gareau of Montreal, the first woman to cross the finish line behind Ruiz, was invited back to Boston to receive the victory wreath. "I feel bad for her," was all that Gareau would say about Ruiz.

Looking back, the facts are now well known: Ruiz did not run all of the New York Marathon in 1979. She did not run all of the Boston Marathon in 1980.

Why did Ruiz do it?

Nobody knows for sure. Some people claim that she did it for the acclaim she knew she'd receive. After her marathon in New York, the president of the company where Ruiz worked, a marathon runner himself, applauded her for her fine effort. He offered to pay her expenses to Boston for the marathon there. Ruiz accepted the offer.

This theory has it that Ruiz didn't intend to actually win at Boston. All she had meant to do was make a good showing, as she had in New York. That would justify the support of her boss and fellow workers. When she jumped out onto the race course, she had no idea that there weren't any women runners in front of her.

Another theory has it that Ruiz did it for the money. She owed more than one thousand dollars to several New York department stores, and they were pressuring her for payment.

Ruiz knew that winning the Boston marathon could be worth a great deal. There is no direct payment to the winner since the marathon is an event for amateur athletes. But being a nationally known celebrity, the winnner of any top-rated marathon is offered money to make public appearances.

For instance, just a few hours after the Boston Marathon in 1980, Ruiz received an offer from a Long Island businessman. He said he would pay her ten thousand dollars if she would run the thirty miles between the two restaurants he owned. A race track offered to pay Ruiz to run a competition with a harness horse. Ruiz turned down both offers.

Despite the evidence against her, Ruiz continued to proclaim her innocence. Through her lawyer, she said, "I won Boston. I ran New York. I never lied."

Officials of the Boston Marathon asked her to return the winner's medal she had received after crossing the finish line. Ruiz refused.

Rosie Ruiz wasn't the only runner disqualified following the 1980 Boston Marathon. Michael R. Weiler, age twenty-four, of North Miami, Florida, was disqualified after officials discovered his race number — seventy-eight — appeared in the spotters' record only at the final checkpoint, about five miles from the finish line. Weiler was the twenty-eighth runner to cross the finish line.

It was not the first time that Weiler had been involved in road-race cheating. He was also disqualified at the Orange Bowl Marathon in January 1980 and the Gasparilla Classic in Tampa, Florida.

Weiler was once interviewed by *The Miami Herald*. "I have never cheated in a race in my life," he told the interviewer.

Rosie Ruiz has described the year that followed the 1980 Boston Marathon as being "very difficult." She received several threatening telephone calls, was sued on charges of writing bad checks (the suit was settled out of court), and she changed jobs and apartments.

T-shirts that served to make fun of her were seen frequently. One, for example, read: ROSIE RUIZ TRACK CLUB on the front, along with a picture of a big subway token.

A race promoter in Moline, Illinois, sought to schedule a "Rosie Ruiz Marathon." A competitor could jump into the six-mile race a short distance from the finish and still receive a T-shirt.

As far as anyone knows, Ruiz did not compete in any running events in the year following her appearance in Boston. During the summer of 1980, she entered the Green Mountain Island Marathon in South Hero, Vermont. But shortly before the race, she withdrew. She said that she had tripped on a curbstone while running in New York City and had injured her hip.

In the weeks leading to the Boston Marathon in 1981, Rosie Ruiz's name was heard often.

Will Cloney, the race director, was asked a hundred times, "What are you doing to prevent another Rosie Ruiz?"

Cloney's reply was always the same. "There are at least six people at every checkpoint, some who do nothing but check the women. There are several unidentified checkers at strategic points along the route. There are a couple of electronic gimmicks to fall back on. There's not a chance in the world there will be another Rosie."

Several weeks before the 1981 race, Cloney issued Ruiz an invitation. Allison Roe of New Zealand won the Boston Marathon in 1981. Rosie Ruiz was not heard from.

4

Baseball's Zany Hoaxers

Early in the 1981 baseball season, the Oakland A's faced the Seattle Mariners at the Kingdome. Not long before the game began, A's manager Billy Martin, standing on the dugout steps, happened to look toward home plate. What he saw caused his brow to wrinkle.

He went out for a closer look. Sure enough, the batter's box seemed longer than it should be. Martin summoned an umpire who agreed that something was wrong. When the umpire had the box measured, it was found to be seven feet long, not the regulation six feet.

The umpire questioned the groundskeeper who had put down the lines. The man admitted he had tampered with the dimensions on orders from Maury Wills, the manager of the Mariners. Wills, in turn, was forced to admit that he had ordered the change. He said he did it because the A's were complaining that one of his players was stepping out of the box toward the mound as he batted.

When Wills's trick was discovered, he looked ridiculous in the eyes of his baseball colleagues.

He also suffered by being suspended for two days and fined five hundred dollars.

Not long after, Wills was dismissed as the manager of the Mariners. No one knows for certain how much of a part the batter's box incident played in Wills's dismissal (the Mariners had lost eighteen of twenty-four games under Wills). But it was undoubtedly a factor, making it one of the most costly hoaxes — or attempted hoaxes — in baseball history.

Incidents such as this one involving Maury Wills are seldom seen today. Every team once had its share of tricksters and hoaxers; nowadays they're a rare breed.

There used to be more laughs in baseball. Players tried hard to win, but they managed to have fun, too. Money has made the difference. The enormous sums paid players today has made them more businesslike about their profession.

A player who is earning several thousand dollars a day is not going to disappear from his team for a week or so. A modern-day player would never risk injury by trying to catch a baseball dropped from the Washington monument. But these things happened in the past.

Players of the past could run, throw, and hit about on a par with players today. But more than a few of them were also colorful and amusing men, always ready to attempt a trick or hoax. The spirit of baseball is poorer without them.

One such figure was Rube Waddell. A big, loose, lanky pitcher, Waddell is one of the great folk heroes of baseball. He not only pitched with stunning speed but he threw an extraordinary curve ball.

Except for his willingness to abandon his team whenever the spirit moved him, Waddell might be ranked as one of the top three or four pitchers of all time. He would take off for any one of a number of reasons — to go fishing, serve as a drum major in a town band, wrestle alligators, or tend bar. He once skipped the club to play marbles with some children.

It often has been written that Waddell, in the late innings of a game, would call in his outfielders, instructing them to sit on the bench. He would then get the batters to strike out or hit harmless grounders. Since the rules provide that nine men must be on the field at all time, the story is undoubtedly mythical. In exhibition games, however, Waddell would sometimes tell his outfielders to sit down, and then proceed to strike out the side.

The season of 1904 was perhaps Waddell's best. A member of the Philadelphia A's at the time, Waddell won twenty-six games and struck out three hundred forty-three batters. In one game that season, he sent sixteen batters down swinging. Whenever it was announced that Waddell was going to pitch, huge crowds filled the stands.

Players on opposing teams tried to figure out ways to beat Waddell. A pitcher for the St. Louis Browns had an idea. He would seek to get Waddell tired before a game he was to pitch. Then he wouldn't be able to throw with his usual effectiveness.

Before the game in question, the Browns pitcher started an argument with Rube. "I know you can throw the ball hard," the pitcher said. "But I can throw farther than you can."

Rube laughed at the man. "I'll *bet* I can," said the pitcher. Rube agreed to a small wager.

The two men trudged out to deep center field. The competition involved throwing the ball toward home plate. The St. Louis pitcher threw first. The ball traveled only as far as second base. Then Rube wound up and let the ball fly. It soared over second base and landed several feet in front of home plate.

The St. Louis pitcher realized immediately he was overmatched, but his mind was working. "Let's make it the best four out of seven," he said. That was fine with Rube, who put his next three throws in the vicinity of home plate.

The St. Louis pitcher pretended to be astonished. "That's amazing, Rube," he said. "Can you do that again?" Rube was happy to demonstrate that he could. Before the session was over, the St. Louis pitcher enticed Rube to throw again, and again, and again — as many as forty or fifty times.

Eventually, the pitcher handed the money over to Rube. The players went to their respective dugouts to await the start of the game, the St. Louis pitcher laughing to himself.

That afternoon Waddell was his usual unbeatable self, striking out fourteen batters and breezing to an easy win. The St. Louis pitcher was amazed that his trick hadn't worked. On his way to the clubhouse after the game, Waddell saw the St. Louis pitcher who had engaged him in the throwing contest. "Hey," said Rube, "thanks for the workout. That was swell practice."

Waddell pitched for the A's until 1908, when he was traded to the St. Louis Browns. His fast ball wasn't quite as fast as it once had been, and his curve was no longer quite as awesome. But Rube still managed to win nineteen games.

The Browns wanted to keep him out of trouble during the off-season, so they actually employed him to go hunting, which he loved to do. Each week he would go off into the woods in quest of game, and return to the St. Louis office on Saturday to pick up his salary. He was paid a sufficient amount to last him through the week, and always in one-dollar bills.

It was a perfect arrangement for both parties. Rube had a chance to go hunting all the time and he was never without money. The St. Louis team always knew where he was and what he was doing.

In 1910, after he had completed the season with a record of three wins and one defeat, Rube realized that his major league career was finished. But he felt he still could pitch in the minor leagues. He signed on with Minneapolis of the American Association, and remained with the club for three years. He worked as spot pitcher, that is, he was used chiefly in critical situations. He helped Minneapolis win three pennants in that role.

One season, Rube helped the team in an unusual way. Minneapolis was in the thick of the pennant race and preparing to face the Toledo Mud Hens in a critical three-day, four-game series.

"We've got to figure out a way to handle that guy Yingling," the Minneapolis manager said to the team not long before the first game of the series. Yingling was Toledo's best pitcher. "If we can beat him," the manager declared, "we should be able to take the series and keep our lead."

"Leave Yingling to me, boss," said Waddell. "He won't bother us."

The next day, with the series opener scheduled, Waddell failed to show up at the ballpark. Yingling, the Toledo pitcher, was also absent. Both men didn't appear the following day, a Saturday, nor on Sunday, when a doubleheader was scheduled. Minneapolis didn't miss Rube too much, because he was only expected to serve as a relief hurler, but the Toledo manager was livid that his star pitcher missed the entire series.

The day after Toledo left town, Waddell strolled into the Minneapolis dressing room. He was carrying a string of fish. "Where have you been?" roared the Minneapolis manager.

"Taking care of Yingling like I promised," Rube answered. "He didn't show up, did he? Here, boss, have some fish. I've got plenty of my own."

Rube continued to explain. "I took Yingling out to Lake Minnetonka for some fishing. Our luck was so good, we decided to stay as long as the fish were biting. That Yingling sure loves to fish."

Rube's manager shook his head from side to

side. The important thing was that Minneapolis had swept the four-game series against Toledo. He decided he wouldn't make an issue of Rube's absence.

But a few weeks later, the Minneapolis ball club got a whopping bill from a local fish market for fish that Rube had purchased.

He and Yingling had never gone fishing at all. Where *did* they go? To this day, nobody knows.

Al Schacht's baseball career was quite forgettable. A pitcher for the old Washington Senators from 1919-1921, Schacht never won more than six games in a season and finished with a lifetime record of fourteen wins, ten defeats.

But Schacht was more of a clown than a pitcher, and his antics on the diamond often brought waves of laughter from the stands. After his major league career ended, Schacht drifted back to the minors to play for Reading in the New York-Pennsylvania League. As a member of the Reading team, he would sometimes entertain the fans before a game or during the intermission between games of a doubleheader. The San Diego chicken does the same thing today. But the chicken doesn't also pitch; Schacht did.

One day Reading was scheduled to play Scranton. Before the game, Schacht amused the spectators with a game of "baseball-golf" that he had invented. The game involved a sawdust-filled baseball. He could hammer the ball with all his might, but it never traveled past second base. Schacht would whack the ball so it landed on one of the basepaths, then, using a bat as a golfer uses a putter, he would tap the ball toward an imaginary "hole."

When the show was over and the game was about to begin, Schacht stuffed the sawdust ball into his pocket and ambled out to the bullpen, ready to be called upon if needed.

It was a tight game, and when Reading's starting pitcher weakened in the ninth inning, Schacht was called upon. As he was taking his warm-up throws, he realized that the sawdust baseball was still in his back pocket. A grin crossed his face. Here was the opportunity for some real fun.

When he had finished warming up, Schacht called his catcher to the mound. "Look, I've still got the goofy baseball," Schacht said, whereupon he pulled it from his pocket, replacing it with the regulation ball. "From the first pitch on," Schacht said to the catcher, "get the ball back to me as fast as you can. Don't let the umpire see it!"

The catcher knew it was useless to argue with the zany Schacht. He nodded and returned to his position behind the plate. Schacht prepared to throw, looking in for the signal. The catcher put down two fingers, meaning a curve ball. But he had no idea of what kind of pitch Schacht was going to throw.

Joe Boley, who later would play for Philadelphia in the American League, was at the plate. Boley was a solid hitter, known for his sizzling line drives. He dug in, eyeing Schacht carefully.

Schacht went into his windup and served the ball chest-high and right over the heart of the plate. Boley couldn't have been happier. He unleashed his powerful swing and met the ball solidly.

Whap! There was the sound a wet towel makes when it is thrown to the floor. The ball lifted harmlessly into the air and settled into Schacht's waiting glove. Boley was shaking his head from side to side as he trudged to the dugout.

Schacht could see at a glance that the sawdust ball had been knocked lopsided by Boley's bat. He turned his back to the plate and began kneading it back into shape.

When the ball was round again, Schacht prepared to face the next batter, Fred Stiles. Once again Schacht sent a perfect pitch up to the plate. Stiles teed off with a home-run swing. *Whap!* Again the ball landed harmlessly in Schacht's glove.

Schacht turned his back to the plate again and began working on the battered ball. Not only had it been knocked lopsided again, but some of the stitches had parted. Schacht hoped the ball would last only long enough to get the third out of the inning.

Rube Parnham, a capable hitter, was the next batter. Schacht delivered; Parnham swung hard. This time the ball fluttered toward Schacht like a wounded sparrow, dribbling bits of sawdust as it traveled.

Parnham was enraged. "That guy's throwing a trick ball!" he screamed at the umpire.

The umpire didn't need Parnham to tell him that. He raced to the mound and demanded to see the ball.

"It's the trick ball," Schacht said with a sheepish grin. But he had already cooked up a story to pacify the umpire.

"Listen, ump," he continued, "I got Boley and Stiles out with real baseballs. Then I saw Parnham coming to bat, and I decided to have some fun. You know how he's always 'popping off' around the clubhouse. I just wanted to show him up, that's all."

Schacht could see he had a fighting chance. "Let Parnham bat over again," he urged. "I'll use the real baseball."

"Okay," said the umpire. "But no more tricks."

Schacht had gotten away with the hoax. But Parnham was furious that Schacht had made him the butt of one of his jokes. He lashed the bat back and forth as he waited for the pitch. Schacht sent a slow, wide-breaking curve ball up to the plate. Parnham swung with vengeance, and popped the ball up to the pitcher.

In *The Official Encyclopedia of Baseball*, there's a line of type beneath the name "Charles Victor Faust" that testifies he was a pitcher for the New York Giants, and that he appeared in two games during the season of 1911. But the entry is only partly true. Faust did wear a Giants uniform and take the mound for two appearances that year, but to say that he was a pitcher, or even to claim that he was a professional baseball player, is to be guilty of stretching the truth. Faust played quite a different role.

Faust, a slender young man with a pointed chin and a long, thin nose, first became known to the Giants early in the 1911 season. One April afternoon before a game in St. Louis, Faust entered the Giants dugout and introduced himself to manager John McGraw. He told McGraw of a strange happening. A fortune-teller in Kansas City had predicted that if he were to pitch for the Giants, the team would win the National League championship.

Many baseball people were superstitious in those days. They feared jinxes. They carried good luck charms. If a team was on a winning streak, some players would wear the same clothes day after day, eat the same foods, and follow the same routine. John McGraw was no exception. When he heard the mention of "fortune-teller," his interest perked up. He told Faust to grab a glove and ball and throw a few pitches.

Faust, wearing his dress suit, marched out to the pitcher's mound. McGraw assigned a catcher to go behind the plate. As soon as Faust went into his windup, McGraw could see he was no pitcher. His arms and legs flapped wildly. His fastball had no speed. His curve failed to break.

"What do you think, Mr. McGraw?" Faust asked when he had finished.

McGraw was grim-faced. "Let's see you hit a few," he said.

Faust grabbed a bat and hurried to the plate. Several of the New York players had gathered around by the time and decided to have some fun. They took up positions in the field as Faust prepared to swing.

The batting practice pitcher threw a soft pitch over the heart of the plate about letter high. Faust swung and missed. He swung a second time without making contact. On the third pitch, Faust topped a slow roller down the third-base line. Darting in, the third baseman pretended to fumble the ball. While he was trying to pick it up, Faust rounded first base and headed for second.

As he went sliding in, the second baseman pretended to commit an error, letting the ball go through him and into center field. Faust got to his feet and started running again. He never stopped until he went sliding across home plate.

McGraw and a number of players slapped him on the back. Faust grinned from ear to ear. The fact that he had ruined an expensive suit didn't bother him at all.

When the Giants left St. Louis, Faust went with them. McGraw had a hunch that he was going to bring the team good luck. Faust was given a uniform and provided with spending money. Every day he would go to the mound and warm up as if he expected to pitch. The players encouraged him. "You're looking good out there," they'd say to him, or "Your fastball's really hummin'."

McGraw went along with the hoax to the extent of having Faust made an official member of the team for two games. He pitched one inning in each of those games, and allowed one run in the second game.

At the plate, he was more of a success. The record book shows that he stole two bases and scored a run.

But it was as a good luck charm that Faust excelled. The Giants won the pennant in 1911. Faust was with the team again in 1912 and 1913.

The Giants were champions of the National League both years.

After the 1913 season, Faust went to McGraw and told him he wasn't feeling well. When his health did not improve, the Giants offered to send him on a vacation so he might be well enough to join the team the next spring. But Faust was too sick. He did not appear in a Giant uniform in 1914. That was the year the "Miracle Braves" of Boston, in last place on July 4th, zoomed from the cellar to capture the pennant.

Charles Victor Faust never got to serve as a New York Giant good luck charm again. He died on June 18, 1915.

In the twelve years during the early 1900s that he played with an assortment of teams in both the American and National League, Charles (Gabby) Street earned a reputation as a catcher without equal. He could hang on to anything any pitcher threw. He even handled the terrifying fastballs of the famous Walter Johnson with ease.

Gabby was also outstanding when it came to catching pop foul flies. When he threw off his mask, got a bead on the ball, and planted himself beneath it, the hitter would invariably toss his bat away and head for the dugout. No one could even remember when the sure-handed Street had bobbled a pop-up.

In the years that he played for the Washington Senators, one of Street's most vocal supporters was Pres Gibson, a newspaper reporter. Gibson declared that anyone who could make child's play of Walter Johnson's pitches, as Street did, could handle any pitcher in baseball. In addition, said Gibson, Street could glove pop-ups that no other catcher in baseball could hold.

One day, Gibson got into an argument with a fan concerning Street's skills. "I don't care how high the ball goes," Gibson declared, "if Gabby can get near the ball, he'll hold on to it."

"How about a ball that goes one hundred feet into the air?" asked the fan.

"Make that two hundred or three hundred feet, and Gabby will still get it," Gibson said.

"Let's see," said the fan, "the Washington Monument is some five hundred feet in height. Do you think Street could catch a ball dropped from the top of the Washington Monument?"

Gibson hesitated, but only for a second. "Sure!" he declared.

"I'll bet he can't," said the fan.

"You're on!" answered Gibson.

So it was that on the afternoon of August 21, 1908, that a strange scene unfolded at the base of the Washington Monument. A large crowd gathered. Street took up a position near the monument's base, nervously pounding his favorite mitt. He looked up the tall, tapered shaft of white marble, hoping to be able to catch a glimpse of Gibson, who had taken a box of baseballs to the monument's five hundred-foot level, where eight small windows, two on each side, were located.

Street began to have doubts about what he was doing. A ball falling five hundred feet would gather tremendous speed. If he misjudged it and the ball struck him, he could be seriously injured. But he realized he could not back out now. He braced himself for the first of Gibson's tosses, peering up toward the small windows.

When the first ball was tossed, the crowd oohed and aahed. At about the halfway point of its descent, it hit the side of the monument, then caromed crazily far out of Street's reach. The same thing happened on the next two tosses.

Gibson realized what was wrong; it was the wind. So, after relaying his plans to Street and giving him time to change position, Gibson went to the windows on the opposite face of the monument, and resumed throwing.

But the wind still played tricks with the ball, carrying it beyond Street's reach, although once he barely missed making the catch. Finally, Gibson had only one baseball remaining. He looked down at Street, a tiny speck surrounded by more than a hundred other tiny specks. Gibson let the last baseball fly. He watched as Street adjusted his position, saw him camp under it, spreading his feet wide.

Down the ball plummeted. Street reached out. The ball slammed into the glove with a loud clap. The crowd roared its approval. Street had made the catch.

While a skilled glove man, Gabby Street was never a star during his career. Ordinary is a good word to describe him. Yet Street became a famous man that August afternoon in 1908. For the rest of his life, total strangers would come up to him and ask to shake the hand of the player that had caught a baseball dropped from the top of the Washington Monument.

At the spring training camp of the Brooklyn

Dodgers several years later, a group of players were discussing Street's amazing feat. One of the players wondered whether it would be possible to catch a baseball dropped from an airplane. The players decided to try it.

They hired an aviator of the day, a young woman named Ruth Law, to pilot a rickety, two-seated biplane over the ballpark. Jim Kelly, the trainer for the Brooklyn team, would ride along and drop the ball while the plane circled the field.

The Dodgers were a zany team and treated the stunt as a big joke. When the plane came clattering over the field, they grabbed their mitts and raced under it, laughing and shouting. Among the "fielders" was Dodger manager Wilbert Robinson, who was having more fun than anyone.

As Robinson and the others looked skyward, they saw a round object come sailing out of the plane. Several of the players raced over to the spot where they expected it to come down. Robinson got there first. "I've got it! I've got it!" he cried. The other players pulled back, allowing Robinson to make the catch.

The wind was blowing hard and that fact, combined with the tremendous speed at which the object was traveling, caused Robinson to misjudge it at the last moment. The object caromed off the heel of his glove to smack him squarely in the chest.

Robinson let out a blood-curdling scream. The object had broken open, drenching Robinson's upper body with juice and pulp. For some reason, Jim Kelly had tossed a grapefruit instead of a baseball.

46

5

Ringer

A ringer, says the dictionary, is a racehorse, athlete, or the like that is dishonestly substituted for another in a competitive event. A fast horse is substituted for a slow one. A skilled and experienced professional boxer replaces an amateur. A student entices a brighter friend to take an exam for him. A ringer who gets away with the deception usually turns certain defeat or failure into victory or success.

In the case of horse racing, the use of a ringer can be very profitable. A fortune can be made by secretly substituting a champion horse for one of modest talents.

For years there were rumors of ringer artists at work at small race tracks in Florida and New England. But in 1977, big time racing fell victim to such a hoax.

On September 23 that year, a dark and rainy Friday, a horse named Lebon won the ninth race at New York's Belmont Park, one of the most renowned race courses in the United States. Spectators gasped in amazement when lights flashed on the electronic information board in the track infield to report that a two-dollar bet on Lebon was worth one hundred sixteen dollars. It was one of the biggest payoffs of the year in New York.

According to *The Racing Form*, a newspaper specializing in information about horses and their past races, Lebon's record was a dismal one. From the small South American country of Uruguay, Lebon had not won a race in ten months. When Lebon had raced at Belmont Park earlier in September, the horse had finished eleventh.

In all of 1976, Lebon had won only seven hundred eleven dollars, not nearly enough money to keep the animal in oats. Anyone who believed that the horse named Lebon had a chance to win the ninth race at Belmont Park on September 23, 1977, might also have believed in the Easter bunny or the tooth fairy.

But there was at least one man who had faith in Lebon that afternoon, and bet heavily. The man's name was Mark Gerard. In the minutes following the race, the forty-three-year-old Gerard, a well known race track veterinarian, presented more than two dozen winning fifty-dollar tickets to a track cashier.

The cashier counted the tickets and figured their value. They were worth $77,900. The cashier didn't have that much money on hand so he sent a messenger to get more.

The cashier examined the tickets again to be sure that they weren't counterfeit. Then he counted out the money, bundled it with thick elastic bands, put the bundles in a brown paper bag, and handed the bag to Dr. Gerard.

The cashier then offered to hail a security guard as an escort for Dr. Gerard, but he refused the offer. He flipped a few bills to the cashier as a tip, tucked the bag under his arm, and hurried away.

All of what had happened concerning Lebon, and how the horse happened to be entered in the ninth race at Belmont Park on September 23, 1977, may never be known. But some facts are clear, and together they make a bizarre tale.

Lebon was not the only horse that Dr. Gerard had purchased in Uruguay. He had also arranged to buy Cinzano, a Uruguayan champion. Cinzano had run in eight races in Uruguay; the horse had won seven of those eight races. The one time the horse was defeated, he was bumped and badly injured. Nevertheless, he still managed to finish second.

On the evening of June 3, 1977, Cinzano and Lebon, along with six Argentinian horses, were loaded aboard a plane at the airport in Carrasco, Uruguay. After stopping at Tocumen Airport in Panama City, Panama, to pick up another horse, the plane continued to Kennedy Airport in New York. The horses were being imported to the States to be sold there.

Papers that were examined by an official of the Animal Health Division of the U.S. Department of Agriculture, the agency of the federal government that supervises the importation of most animals, showed that Dr. Gerard had paid sixteen hundred dollars for Lebon and eighty-one thousand dollars for Cinzano.

In other papers that accompanied the horses, Lebon was described as a five-year-old bay of reddish-brown coloring with a white spot on its forehead. Cinzano was listed as a bay four-year-old, also with a white spot on its forehead. But in Cinzano's case, the spot was lower, longer, running down between the eyes, and more irregular in shape than Lebon's. No photographs were sent with the horses.

Blood samples were taken from the horses to make sure they were not suffering from any contagious disease, and later the animals were shipped to the quarantine station in Clifton, New Jersey, that is operated by the U.S. Department of Agriculture. Such precautions are necessary to protect American animals from becoming disease-infected. After more testing, Lebon and Cinzano were declared free of disease and released from the quarantine station. Dr. Gerard arranged for the two horses to be taken by van to stables he owned in Muttontown, Long Island. The horses arrived there on June 11, 1977. Dr. Gerard had by this time negotiated a sale for one of the horses — Cinzano — to an American horse racer.

The next evening, the horse named Cinzano was reported to have reared up in its stall, struck its head, suffered a fractured skull and a broken ankle, and died. Dr. Gerard called another veterinarian and asked him to sign the death certificate for the horse.

Later the veterinarian would admit that he had never seen the dead horse. He had signed the certificate as a favor to a fellow vet. All that Dr. Gerard had shown him was a leg that came from a horse. What horse was it? The veterinarian could not say for sure.

The horse's body was removed from its stall

and deposited in the Huntington, New York, town dump. Soon it was covered with many thousands of tons of garbage. Joseph Taub, the New Jersey computer executive who had purchased Cinzano from Dr. Gerard filed an insurance claim when he learned of the horse's death and collected a full premium from the insurance company.

New York state regulations do not permit track veterinarians to race horses that they own. But Dr. Gerard knew how to sidestep that rule.

He sought out a trainer named Jack Morgan. His father had been a trainer, and thirty-two-year-old Morgan had been around horses all his life. After Army service, including duty in Viet Nam, Morgan had gone to work for Gerard, managing his office affairs. He worked for Gerard for nine years, quitting in a dispute over salary.

Next, Morgan started training horses and was beginning to be successful. It was at this point that Dr. Gerard approached him and asked him for a favor. The favor was to take over a horse that Gerard had imported from Uruguay called Lebon. In return, Gerard promised to say good things about Morgan in racing circles, thus helping him to get more horses to train.

Morgan had been training the horse for only a week when Dr. Gerard told Morgan to race him. Morgan said no; the horse wasn't ready to race. Dr. Gerard insisted. Morgan had no choice but to agree. He entered the horse in a race at Belmont Park. The date was September 9.

American racing officials go to considerable lengths to prevent one horse from being substituted for another in a race. Each horse is given a serial number, which is tattooed on the animal's inner lip. Horses are also identified by their "night eyes," the horny growths on the legs that correspond to fingerprints in humans.

Before every race a horse enters, his or her lip tattoo and night eyes are carefully checked. But Uruguay does not use lip tattoos or register night eyes. All the New York racing officials had to go on in the case of the horse named Lebon was description of the horse's markings, chiefly the white spot on its forehead.

In the race on September 9, Morgan's opinion of the horse proved correct. The horse finished eleventh.

Under Morgan's supervision, the horse grew healthier, eating better and galloping faster. Morgan told Dr. Gerard that the horse was ready to win. He entered the horse in the ninth race at Belmont Park on September 23.

The horse won. Dr. Gerard traded in his winning tickets for the brown paper bag filled with cash.

The story might have ended at that point, and Dr. Gerard might have gone about enjoying the money he had won. But in the moments following the race, a photographer snapped the horse's picture.

The picture ended up in a newspaper in Uruguay named *El Pais*. A story accompanying the picture identified the horse as Lebon and hailed him as a "hometown hero" for his victory at the famous Belmont Park.

When those familiar with Uruguayan racing and race horses saw the photograph, they realized at once it was not Lebon; it was Cinzano.

Authorities in Uruguay notified New York racing officials. An investigation was launched. Soon after, the New York State Racing and Wagering Board suspended the licenses of Dr. Gerard and Morgan. The ban on Morgan was lifted on December 31, 1977, and he was permitted to resume work as a trainer.

The following year, Dr. Gerard was charged with grand larceny for entering a ringer in two races and falsifying an insurance claim. Almost one year to the day of the fateful race, Dr. Gerard's trial began.

Dr. Gerard was defended by cool and suave F. Lee Bailey, one of the most noted criminal lawyers of the day. Bailey admitted to the jury that a switch in horses had taken place.

But then, in a surprise move, Bailey introduced Alice Gerard, Dr. Gerard's wife, as a witness. Alice Gerard testified that it was she who made the switch. What she actually had done, she said, was swap the horses' bridles. The horse wearing Cinzano's bridle had fractured its skull and died. Dr. Gerard testified that he had not known that the bridles had been exchanged and believed that the horse that Morgan was training was Lebon.

Why had Alice Gerard made the switch in bridles? She did it, she said, to embarrass the New York state racing officials. She claimed she intended to write a book about the ringer scheme in an effort to damage the integrity of the sport. Or, as F. Lee Bailey put it, she sought "to wipe the face of racing with a dark and dirty brush."

It is not likely that all the jurors believed Alice Gerard's story. It was pointed out that she had a ten-year history of mental illness.

But she did plant in the jury's mind some doubt as to her husband's guilt. During his seventy-five-minute summation to the jury, Bailey pounded and pounded on the question of reasonable doubt. The jury of six men and six women hardly flexed a muscle as they watched Bailey perform.

In its verdict the jury cleared Dr. Gerard of engineering the ringer scheme. They believed that he learned about the switch "somewhere along the line," but were not convinced he planned it.

Dr. Gerard's body went limp with relief when the jury announced its verdict. "I'd feel better if I weren't convicted of anything, but at least I'm not a horse thief," he said. "They used to hang them."

6
Fall Guys
(and Gals)

There is at least one American sport that is as phony as an eleven-dollar bill. The participants are trained to bluff and fake. Each contest follows a script that is worked out in advance. The spectators fully realize that what they're watching is make-believe.

The sport is popular in small towns and big cities, and regularly fills New York's Madison Square Garden to the rafters. It's leading performers are among the highest paid of all athletes.

The sport, of course, is wrestling (although much of the above description also fits the roller derby).

Not all wrestling is based on fraud, only the professional version. Amateur wrestling, as conducted in high school and colleges, is honorable and upright.

Amateur wrestling features "catch-as-catch can" bouts in which the shoulder must be put in contact with the mat for one second, and then a fall is declared by the referee. Points are scored for takedowns (taking an opponent to the mat and gaining control of him or her), reversals (coming from underneath to gain control of an opponent), near falls (controlling an opponent in a pinning situation), and escapes.

Amateur wrestling, however, has never been an important spectator sport. Matches are dull. Watching amateur wrestling is something like watching bowling or fishing.

But professional wrestling is different. Professional wrestling offers athletic skill and showmanship in equal amounts. It seldom lacks in drama and excitement.

But as for honesty, that's another matter. A sports columnist for a New York daily newspaper once displayed the skill of picking the winners in wrestling bouts. He was never wrong.

Not only was he able to name the winning wrestler, but occasionally he would also predict the particular hold that would end the match and the time of the fall. It was obvious that someone was tipping him off.

One night Jim Londos faced Ray Steele at Madison Square Garden for the heavyweight championship. The day before the bout, the columnist predicted that Londos would win in fifty minutes with his famous airplane spin, and retain his title. Londos did win, but it took fifty-seven minutes. And he overcame Steele, not with an airplane spin, but with a series of flying tackles.

The next day the writer's column was headed, AN APOLOGY TO THE PUBLIC. He said that he was thoroughly embarrassed because he had not reported the time of the fight accurately, being wrong by seven minutes. As for not getting the winning hold right, he said there was absolutely no excuse for that.

In professional wrestling, the bout always presents good vs. evil, hero vs. villain. There is no mistaking either role-player. The villain always wears a bizarre costume, and the hero is clean-cut and wears a saintly expression.

As the referee introduces the opponents in the center of the ring, the villain may either refuse to shake hands or he will grab one of the hero's hands and twist the fingers into knots. Then, while the referee's back is turned, the villain plays dirty tricks on the hero, pulling his hair, kicking him, or strangling him. Remember, the bout hasn't yet begun. The fans scream at the referee, begging him to pay attention to what's happening to the hero.

Cowboy Bill Watts, one of the most noted villains of recent times, once stated that, "Everything I do is to get crowd reaction." Watts was once matched against Don McClarity, a classic good guy. Before the match, McClarity stood on the ring apron and busily signed autographs. When a young woman approached Watts and asked for an autograph, he seized the paper she held out to him and tore it up. The crowd jeered.

A young man raced down the aisle and challenged Watts to a fist fight. Watts stepped out onto the apron, directly over the young man, and motioned him to enter the ring. The crowd went wild. Two policemen grabbed the would-be victim and escorted him to his seat.

Once the match gets underway, the script normally calls for the villain to seize the hero in a

series of torturous holds, with the hero display-
ing agonizing pain. Since the action takes place
in a four-sided ring, all kicks, stomps, butts, and
other blows have to be repeated four times so
that every paying customer can see what's happening.

As the match draws to its conclusion, the
villain picks up the hero, boosts him over his head,
and starts spinning him around, a piece of strategy
known as the airplane spin. As a finale, he slams
the hero to the canvas. The hero lies there, acting like a man who has been tossed from the roof
of a forty-story building.

To win a fall, which, like a round in boxing, is
a timed segment of the match, one wrestler must
hold or force the shoulders of the other against
the mat for three seconds. But the villain ne-
glects to do this. Instead, he parades about the
ring, gloating over his victory. Boos and catcalls
rain down upon him. Some people throw things.

Unnoticed by the villain, the hero, who has
been left for dead, begins to move. As the crowd
supports him with their cheers, he staggers to his
feet. The villain is struck with terror. He cries
for mercy. The hero is in no mood to be merciful.
He bangs the villain to the canvas with a flying
tackle and quickly pins him.

There can be variations to the theme, of course.
If the villain is a colorful rogue, not out-and-out
wicked, and popular with the fans, he may beat
the hero. He may continue defeating heroes for
month after month. But, eventually, a top-ranked
hero, a wrestler who, besides his heroic posture
is also a top drawing card, will vanquish the vil-

lain. In wrestling, good always triumphs over evil in the end.

The promoter, the individual who stages the bout, decides in advance who will be the villain and who will be the hero. He also establishes the length of the match.

The script doesn't have to be long. One promoter, for example, sent this telegram to one of his wrestlers: "Moon tonight in 55 with a flying tackle blowoff." The term "moon tonight" meant that the wrestler was to lose, that is, look at the moon (lie on his back). ". . . in 55" was the length of the bout, fifty-five minutes. The term "blowoff" referred to the finish, the climax, the final hold.

Wrestling's foremost stars get a percentage of the gate receipts and earn more than a quarter of a million dollars a year. But the wrestlers in the supporting matches work on a salary, and rarely make more than five hundred dollars a week.

The difference between a top-flight wrestler and a mere journeyman has little to do with relative skill. It's a matter of showmanship. Wrestlers spend much more time devising gimmicks or characters to improve their acts than they do trying to perfect their half-nelsons or airplane spins.

Antonio Rocca, one of professional wrestling's all-time greats, developed his trademark — bare feet — by accident. When he arrived in New York from his native Argentina, no one could find him a pair of size 13½ sneakers. He had to take part in his first bout barefoot. A press agent sent out a story that Rocca had developed his skill as a wrestler by wrestling wild bulls barefoot. The image fit, so Rocca wore shoes only when he had to, and never in the ring.

A wrestling match should not be looked upon as something competitive. It is more like a carefully rehearsed dance routine.

Professionals know how to work "loose" when putting a hold on an opponent. For example, a man can appear to be tearing an opponent's head off with a headlock, all his muscles straining, and yet the "victim" will hardly be feeling the pressure of his arms.

Many punches never land. As one wrestler throws a punch, the other slaps his thigh. The punch misses by a fraction of an inch, but the spectators are fooled by the victim, who acts like he's been walloped by a sledge hammer, and the sound of the thigh slap.

When one wrestler hoists another over his head to slam him to the mat, he will prolong his hold until the man in the air can brace his body for the landing. And the thrower always tosses his opponent so he lands feet first, so he won't get hurt.

In many matches, as one man lies helpless, the other leaps into the air and stamps on him with one foot. Such conduct never fails to enrage the spectators. But the supposed victim isn't being hurt at all. His opponent breaks the impact of his descent by landing on the other foot first. The foot that seems to be doing the stomping barely touches the victim's belly.

There's similar deception involved in the belly bounce, in which one opponent bounces up and down on the other until he beats him into submission. When the bouncer lands, he always remembers to cushion the impact by hitting the mat with hands first.

Eye-gouging is total fakery. The gouger only presses his bent thumbs against his opponent's brow bones. The flying tackle isn't nearly as devastating as it appears. If it were, an opponent could simply step out of the tackler's way; instead, he stands there.

The airplane whirl is another piece of nonsense. When the victim is released, he stumbles about the ring drunkenly as he attempts to recover his sense. But why doesn't the other wrestler ever get dizzy? He goes around, too, every time the victim does.

If, by accident, a hold should become painful, the victim taps his tormentor with a finger on the leg. This is the standard signal to lay off, because of all the noise in the arena.

One of wrestling's most gruesome sights is blood streaming down a man's face. But if it is real blood, something has gone wrong. Wrestlers rely on a trick developed by Hollywood special effects experts to produce fake blood. Before a bout, one of the contestants will pop a small capsule of red dye into his mouth, holding it in his cheek in the early stages of the match.

At the right moment, after what appears to be a heavy blow, he bites down on the capsule, releasing the dye. He then falls to the mat and covers his face with his hands. As he does so, he smears the red dye over his face. When he gets to his feet, he looks like a man who has just poked his face through a plate glass window. The crowd, revolted by the sight of the man, screams at him to seek revenge.

Sometimes the wrestler who is designated to bleed will tape a dye-filled capsule to his head or neck. The opponent's fist or forearm will shatter the capsule, causing the red liquid to flow.

Sometimes the acting is of extremely high quality. Herman Hickman, rated as one of the top professionals some years ago, once recalled a bout he had against Jim Londos for the heavyweight championship with an ending in which he displayed acting skills that should have won him an Academy Award. It was arranged in advance that the bout would last fifty minutes with Hickman losing. The climax called for Hickman to take a dive from the elevated ring platform out amidst the spectators, whereupon he would be counted out.

Hickman described the bout's final moments as he prepared to finish off the staggering champion: "I backed into the ropes to get more spring for my final assault. As I dove through the air, Londos fell flat to the mat. I sailed out of the ring, going between the second and third rows."

Hickman had been aiming at soft laps in a row of ringside seats, but he missed his target completely. He landed flat on his back on the ground on a lighted cigar butt. He had to lie there while the referee counted to twenty over his motionless body. He could feel the cigar burning his skin. But he never moved a muscle.

The moment he heard the word twenty, Hickman rolled over on his face. Someone dumped a bucket of ice water on him and then three or four people dragged him from the arena. Hickman had played his role to perfection. And he would forever have a big scar on his back from the lighted cigar. He accepted it as evidence of his acting ability.

Are bouts *ever* on the level? Does one wrestler ever make a genuine effort to prevail over an opponent? It does happen. But when it does, it's an accident.

In a bout at Madison Square Garden in New York a number of years ago, the contestants actually tried to hurt one another. This so surprised the audience that they rioted. It took more than a hundred policemen and ushers to stop it.

It began with a standard "tag match" between Antonino Rocca and Edouard Carpentier vs. "Doctor" Jerry Graham and Dick "Bruiser" Afflis. In a tag match, only one member of each team is permitted in the ring at a time. The other stands outside the ropes. When the man in the ring grows weary or starts taking a thrashing, he gets his partner to take his place by tagging him.

In the match in question, Rocca and Carpentier were cast as the heroes. They won the first fall despite gouges, groin kicks, and other sneaky fouls by Graham and Afflis, the villains. They were on their way to winning a second fall in the match when Rocca got Afflis in a "back breaker" hold, slinging him across his back at shoulder level like a sack of meal and preparing to hurl him into the laps of ringside spectators.

Suddenly, Afflis's partner, Doctor Graham, broke the rules by charging into the ring. He began pummeling Rocca about the head, but it was all part of the script. The referee called a foul on Graham and awarded the match to the heroes. The crowd cheered. Graham, still playing his part, continued to rain blows upon Rocca's upper body as the Argentinian donned his robe and prepared to leave the ring.

Just before he climbed through the ropes, Rocca put his hand to his face. When he drew it away, he noticed his fingers were coated with blood. It did not come from any capsule filled with red dye. It was *real* blood.

Rocca lost his temper. He flung off his robe, seized Graham, and began bashing his head against one of the ring posts. Graham started bleeding, and he did not have any dye-filled capsule, either. Ushers and arena policemen climbed into the ring to help Graham, but they could not restrain Rocca. He was like an enraged wild animal.

From the balcony seats, spectators began to toss half-eaten fruit and empty bottles down upon the ring. Hundreds of ground-level fans began surging toward the wrestlers. Wooden chairs were trampled upon and their parts taken as weapons. Clusters of Rocca's fans began to chant, "Get the Bruiser! Get the Bruiser!" as they swept toward the ring.

The first man to enter the ring was wearing an Army jacket and was armed with a furled umbrella. He was soon joined by a second fan who wielded a sharp, pointed stick from a broken chair. Bruiser Afflis charged toward the man with the stick, picked him up, and threw him out of the ring with the ease of a basketball player tossing a free throw. The fan in the Army jacket fled. As other fans entered the ring, Afflis tossed them into the seats. All the while, Rocca was continuing to batter the ring post with Graham's head.

Eventually, New York City police arrived to restore order. They were helped by Rocca who, speaking in Spanish, begged his admirers to restrain themselves. The police were finally able to escort the four wrestlers to their dressing rooms.

Graham did not seem too seriously hurt from the pounding he received. His great sorrow was that a spectator had stolen his five-hundred-dollar, sequin-covered purple robe.

A few days after, Rocca and Graham were each fined one thousand dollars by the State Athletic Commission. For Rocca, who was earning a reported one hundred thousand dollars a year at the time, it was not heavy punishment. But it was a lesson in the folly of losing his temper.

Bruno Sammartino was the most noted wrestler of recent times. From the time he won the heavyweight championship in 1963 until he lost it in 1971, he defended the title 1,063 times. His record at the box office was even more impressive. He chalked up a string of one hundred consecutive sellouts at Madison Square Garden. At the Boston Garden, he never failed to receive a standing ovation when he climbed into the ring.

No matter where he appeared, in the United States or abroad, everyone yelled and screamed at the first sight of Bruno. People climbed on chairs to get a better look or surged toward the ring to touch him. Buttons bearing the words BRUNO POWER, full color portraits of him, and *Bruno* magazines were sold by vendors.

Sammartino stood five-foot-eleven and had a fifty-eight-inch chest. *Sports Illustrated* once called him a "mushroom of muscle." He was born in Italy in 1937, where he skipped school to wrestle in a neighbor's cellar. During World War II, Bruno's home was bombed and he and his family fled to the mountains. The Sammartinos came to the United States when Bruno was fifteen. He suffered from a poor diet and weighed only ninety-three pounds. He started weight-lifting after school and wrestled whenever he could. "It was hard to get competition," he once said. "I beat everyone." He became a professional in 1959 and less than four years later captured the world championship.

Sammartino frequently defended his profession. Wrestlers are not clowns, he protested, but the greatest of athletes. "Football and baseball players are in terrible condition,'" he often said. "In the ring, their tongues would hang out of their mouths.

"I used to idolize these men. Then I found out the truth. They drink, they smoke, they only train a couple of months. Half the year, they rest. Even when playing, they need only short bursts of energy. But in wrestling, you never rest."

Sammartino was highly critical of the media coverage that wrestling received. "Sportswriters disgust me," he once said. "They hardly ever write anything about wrestling, and when they do it's only to make fun or criticize."

As evidence, Sammartino cited his match with Ivan Koloff in which he lost the World Wide Federation championship. Sportswriters joked about the match but none mentioned that he had suffered a shoulder separation. "I could have called the match off," Bruno said, "but I didn't want to disappoint my fans. I had already beaten Koloff four or five times, and if I wasn't in such pain I would have done it again."

Bruno exercised and worked out with weights two hours a day. He watched his diet carefully. He took pride in his reputation. He never smoked or drank in public. He refused to do beer commercials for television.

To those who believed that professional wrestling was merely a bunch of tricks, Bruno offered a great deal of evidence to the contrary. During his career, he suffered eleven broken noses, five shattered ribs, plus dislocated collarbones, wrists, knuckles, and ankles. He was stitched up as regularly as any hockey player.

There are also women wrestlers. The best known is The Fabulous Moohlah, a champion for many years.

At the time of her greatest popularity, The Fabulous Moohlah was fortyish, thick-waisted, with dark wavy hair pulled back off her forehead and falling to her shoulders. She was usually booed or hissed when her name was announced, for the spectators knew that her ring tactics were less than fair and honorable. Wearing a black cape and rainbow-striped wrestling tights, she would parade about the ring, hands on her hips, taunting the crowd.

Before she took the name of The Fabulous Moohlah, the champion was plain Lillian Ellison. She was born and brought up in Columbia, South Carolina. She had twelve brothers. "They used to let me play all the games with them — baseball, football, everything. They used to stuff me inside an old tire and roll me down a hill into a creek."

When Lillian was eight years old, her mother died. To help her take her mind off of her mother's death, Lillian's father tried different methods of entertaining her. One night he took her to a wrestling match. "The minute I saw those girls," Lillian recalls, "I said to him, 'That's what I want to be, a lady wrestler.'"

When she went to high school, Lillian sought out the wrestling coach and asked to try out for the team. The school had no girls' wrestling team and the coach wouldn't permit her to wrestle with the boys. "I told him that didn't make any difference to me," she says. "Finally, he had to let me on the team. He just couldn't stop me, that's all. I wrestled the last two years in high school, but mostly against boys, and beat them, too."

After graduation from high school, Lillian met a wrestling promoter who offered to let her try out in a match. "We're going to have to do something about that name of yours," the promoter said. "Lillian Ellison doesn't sound like a wrestler."

Lillian didn't care what she was called. "All I

want to do is wrestle and make some money," she told the promoter.

The promoter thought for a minute, then said, "You want to make some moohlah, huh? Suppose we call you Slave Girl Moohlah?" That was fine with Lillian.

She wrestled professionally for several weeks, but not with great success. A promoter told her she wasn't big enough. She weighed one hundred eighteen pounds. The promoter told her she needed to put on about twenty pounds.

Lillian returned home and started eating fattening foods. Every morning and every evening she drank a big glass of pure cream with two tablespoons of chocolate syrup and three raw eggs.

After she added, not twenty, but thirty pounds to her frame, she began wrestling again. "At first I wasn't successful," she recalls. "I was too gentle. I wanted everyone to love me.

"Then I realized that's not me. I had to be like I was when I was with my brothers. That's when I finally started to let go."

Lillian won the world championship one night in Baltimore. "They just put thirteen girls in the ring and let them all wrestle at one time," she recalls. "I beat them all. Then I had to wrestle the champion June Byers. I beat her in two straight falls."

After she won the title, the Maryland State Athletic Commission complained to Lillian about her name, Slave Girl Moohlah. They said it was misleading and asked her to change it. One of the officials said, "You beat thirteen girls in one night, and that's pretty fabulous, so let's call you The Fabulous Moohlah." That was fine with Lillian.

Lillian loves professional wrestling. She loves the traveling and meeting people. She loves the money.

But she has had many painful experiences in the ring. She once suffered a broken neck in a match in Denver, an injury that required a long hospital stay and years of treatment after. She has had all her fingers and toes broken at least once. A scar above her upper lip is evidence of the night an opponent rammed her face into the turnbuckle, the metal sleeve that holds the ropes taut. Another time, she had her forehead gashed by the turnbuckle. Her worst injury occurred when a girl jumped on her stomach and damaged her spleen.

"Something like that scares you," says Lillian. "You wonder. But I still love wrestling. It's been good to me. I hope I don't ever lose my title."

Wrestlers such as The Fabulous Moohlah and Bruno Sammartino consider themselves to be not merely athletes, but performers. It's their job to please the spectators. Judging by wrestling's popularity, they've been doing a good job of it.

7

The Fine Art of Fixing

The time: October 1, 1919.
The place: Redland Field, Cincinnati.
The event: Game No. 1 of the World Series, the Cincinnati Reds vs. the Chicago White Sox.

Eddie Cicotte, whose twenty-nine victories during the regular season spearheaded the team's pennant drive, is pitching for the White Sox. A right-hander known for his baffling "shine ball," the thirty-five year-old Cicotte yields a run to the Reds in the first inning.

When Cicotte takes the mound in the fourth inning, with the score tied, one to one, he is ineffective. With one out, Lou Duncan lashes a single to center field; Larry Kopf sends a bouncer to Cicotte. He gloves the ball and throws to second, nailing Duncan.

Then the fireworks begin. Greasy Neale singles over second base. Ivy Wingo laces the ball into right field for another hit. Kopf scores; Neale goes to third. Then Dutch Ruether booms a long drive that caroms off the center-field wall for a triple. Neale and Wingo score easily.

71

Morrie Rath doubles down the left-field line, sending Ruether home. Jack Daubert's single drives in Rath with the fifth Cincinnati run of the inning.

Manager Kid Gleason of the White Sox waves in relief pitcher Roy Wilkinson. Cicotte trudges to the dugout. "The magic right arm that carried the Chicago club through to a pennant had vanished," a newspaper's account of the game would say. The Reds eventually win the game, nine to one.

The underdog Cincinnati team, labeled "a bunch of misfits and outcasts," managed to win the second game, too. After Chicago captured the third game, Cicotte was named to try to get the White Sox even.

He was an improved performer, giving up only five hits, but he made two costly throwing errors in the fifth inning, enabling the Reds to score twice. That was all the runs the Reds got, but that was all they needed, for the White Sox didn't get any at all.

The series was played on a best-of-nine-games basis that year. The Reds wrapped it up in eight.

In the days that followed the final game, several members of the White Sox neglected to come to the club offices to pick up their checks representing their shares of the World Series money. They gave no reason. They simply failed to appear.

But there were plenty of people in baseball who had a good idea of what the reason was. There was open gossip that the series had not been on the level, that certain of the White Sox players had accepted bribes from gamblers to lose the series intentionally.

Charles Comiskey, owner of the White Sox, asked American League president Ban Johnson to investigate the rumors. But there was no investigation.

It was business as usual in 1920. The White Sox were involved in a fight with the Indians and the Yankees for the pennant. But the rumors about the fix continued to be heard.

Toward the end of the season, Hugh Fullerton, a well known sportswriter of the day, decided that it was time for somebody to say out loud what was being whispered and snickered about. Fullerton wrote a series of articles exposing those responsible for the fixed games. *The Chicago American* refused to print the articles. Fullerton took them to *The New York Evening World*. An editor for the *World* revised the articles slightly, then ordered them to be printed under big, black headlines.

Once investigators began looking into the Series, they dredged up one piece of damning information after another. Rube Benton, a pitcher for the New York Giants, was one of the first to reveal what he knew.

Benton said that he heard in the fall of 1919 that there was money to be made by betting on Cincinnati in the Series, because certain White Sox players had been bribed. Benton said that Hal Chase had made forty thousand dollars by betting on the series, thanks to the inside information he had.

As investigators started to dig up things, the

accused players began talking. They talked to newsmen. They talked to a grand jury, which was called into session to determine whether there was sufficient evidence for a trial.

Eddie Cicotte was one of the first of the White Sox to spell out his role in the plot. "[Swede] Risberg, [Chick] Gandil, and [Fred] McMullin were after me for a week," Cicotte declared. "They wanted me to go crooked and I needed the money. I had the wife and two kids — they don't know this and I don't know what they'll think.

"I wanted that ten thousand dollars and I got it. A day before I went to Cincinnati, I put it up to them square: nothing doing unless I got the money. That night I found ten thousand dollars under my pillow. I had sold out [Charles] Comiskey and the boys to pay off the mortgage on the farm for the wife and kids. I wondered what the wife and kids would say if they knew I was a crook."

Cicotte explain how easy it had been to throw the games. "I wasn't putting a thing on the ball," he stated. "You could have read the trademark when I lobbed the ball up to the plate.

"In the fourth game, I deliberately intercepted a throw which might have cut off a run.

"In one of the games, the batter hit a slow grounder to me and I could have made a double play easy. But I was slow, slow enough to let the batter get to first and the runner get to second."

Seven of the White Sox players were eventually brought to trial. They were: Cicotte and Lefty Williams; first baseman Chick Gandil; shortstop

Swede Risberg; third baseman Buck Weaver; and outfielders Happy Felsch and Joe Jackson. These players, all starters and the best two pitchers on the team, have been known ever since as the Black Sox.

An invitation to fix a game today would be greeted by shock. The player approached would almost certainly tell his manager and the team owner. The police would be called in. Of course, there is betting on games today, but there is not the slightest evidence that players are involved in any way.

Besides, it's not practical to try to fix a game today. Many players in baseball receive as much as a quarter- or half-a-million dollars a year. What would it cost to bribe a player earning such a salary? A colossal amount.

Yet gamblers are limited in the amount of money they can bet. Bookmakers seldom accept bets of more than twenty thousand or thirty thousand dollars on a game.

In 1919, it was much different. Players were paid little.

The White Sox, for example, often brooded about the club's tight-fisted owner, Charles Comiskey. Even by standards of the day, Comiskey paid his players poorly. Eddie Cicotte, who had won twenty-eight games in 1917, and twenty-nine in 1919, received a salary of only six thousand dollars, less than half as much as other players of his caliber.

In 1919, Cicotte had a clause in his contract that called for a bonus if he won thirty games.

After he had won twenty-eight, Comiskey refused to let him pitch anymore, saying he had to rest for the World Series.

"So help me, the man was tight," said Chick Gandil, the team's first baseman. "There were many times that the best team in baseball played in filthy uniforms because he hated the idea of paying the cleaning bill. On the road, we ate like cattle.

"I can recall only one real act of generosity on Comiskey's part," Gandil continued. "He sent around a case of champagne after we won the pennant in 1917. Some of us figured it was something the guys up in the press box couldn't use."

Several of the most distressed members of the White Sox asked manager Kid Gleason to go to Comiskey and ask for pay raises on their behalf. Gleason did as the players asked. But Comiskey ignored the request, refusing even to discuss it.

Fixed games, while not common in the days before the World Series scandal of 1919, were not so rare that players had not heard of them. Gamblers had been involved with professional baseball from the sport's earliest days. Players' willingness to cooperate with gamblers in the fixing of games helped to wreck the National Association of Professional Base-Ball Players, a league that was organized in 1875.

No one policed the game. To increase their income, players would make deals with gamblers to arrange the outcome of games. A player might purposely fail to hit in a run-producing situation. Another would commit an error, allowing the opposition to score.

When a game was fixed, the fans sometimes became aware of it. When news of an arranged match did become public, there would be a mad dash for the bookmakers in every league city. The season of 1875 ended with baseball in disrepute, its future clouded by the widespread charges of dishonesty and corruption.

A crusade for honesty began the next year, 1876, when the National League came into existence, replacing the National Association. William Hulbert, who owned and operated the Chicago franchise, was the power behind the crusade.

He began by banning all alcoholic beverages from league parks. "Ladies and children must be allowed to view the competition in a dignified atmosphere," he said.

Hulbert ordered the betting booths at ball park entrances to be torn down. When gamblers were spotted at a game, stadium police routed them from their seats and escorted them outside. Fans stopped adorning the parks with such signs as: NO GAME BETWEEN THESE TWO TEAMS IS TO BE TRUSTED.

Despite Hulbert's efforts, the new league was racked by a gambling scandal in its very first year of operation. It focused on the Louisville Grays, far and away the best team in the league. The Grays were led by pitcher Jim Devlin and outfielder George Hall.

When the Grays, playing at a .667 clip, left on their final road trip of the year, they needed to win only six more games to clinch the championship. They lost their first two contests, arousing Hulbert's suspicions. He sent two investigators to

Hartford, where the Grays were to play the Hartford Blues. The two men watched as the Grays lost, seven to zero, suffering only their second shutout loss of the year.

After another loss and then a tie in Hartford, the Louisville team dropped three straight to the Boston Red Stockings. Things were very serious now. Charles E. Chase, a vice president of the Louisville club, received an anonymous telegram informing him that his players had sold out to gamblers.

The Grays were scheduled to play Cincinnati next. Before the opening game of the series, Chase received another telegram. It said the contest had been fixed and that Louisville was going to lose. In the game, pitcher Devlin, center fielder Hall, and third baseman Al Nichols seemed not to know how to field ground balls, and Louisville did lose.

Hulbert was no longer merely suspicious. He was enraged. He demanded Chase conduct an investigation. When the Louisville vice president questioned Devlin and Hall, they admitted they had played carelessly, but said it was because they were fatigued by the long road trip.

Chase was far from satisfied. He called a team meeting. Since he believed that the gamblers had communicated with the players by telegram, he said he wanted to see duplicates of every telegram sent or received by every Louisville player since the beginning of the season. Any player who failed to authorize Western Union to provide the duplicate messages would be suspended from the team and booted out of the league.

Catcher Bill Craver refused to do what Chase

asked. Everyone else agreed to cooperate — but several kept their fingers crossed.

Within a few days, Chase and Hulbert had the evidence they were seeking. Copies of telegrams revealed that three players — Hall, Devlin, and Nichols — had cooperated with the fixers. They had each sold out for five hundred dollars, and had made twice that amount betting against their teams. No evidence was found against Craver, but he was punished as severely as the guilty players. All four men were expelled from baseball for life.

Hulbert's efforts did not end gambling on baseball or tampering with the outcome of games. In 1878, *The Spirit of the Times* had this to say about baseball in St. Louis: "Baseball, as a professional pastime, has seen its best days in St. Louis. . . . The amount of crooked work that has been done of late is indeed startling, and the game will undoubtedly meet the same fate elsewhere as in St. Louis unless some extra-strong means are taken to prevent it."

In 1882, *The Buffalo Express* recommended that the Buffalo baseball team should "fold up if they can't play a square game."

In 1908, John McGraw, manager of the New York Giants, was accused of offering a bribe to some Philadelphia pitchers to throw games to the New York team. McGraw denied the accusation but the incident was never investigated. "Do nothing and the public will forget," seemed to be baseball's policy in those days.

Hal Chase was another baseball figure often accused of throwing games. Called Prince Hal because of his magnificent skills as a first baseman, Chase joined the New York Highlanders (later to be called the Yankess) in 1910 and later played for Chicago and Cincinnati. The season of 1919 was his last in baseball.

Toward the end of Chase's rookie year, George Stallings, manager of the Highlanders, accused him of throwing games. Chase denied the charge. A hearing followed. Chase was cleared; Stallings was fired.

In 1913, when Frank Chance managed the New York team, he, too, accused Chase of throwing games. Chase denied the accusation again.

In 1918, when Chase was playing for Cincinnati, his manager, Christy Mathewson, one of the most respected figures in the game, accused him of throwing games and suspended him. In a hearing early the following year, three of Chase's teammates testified that Chase had offered them money to throw games. Nevertheless, he was found not guilty by National League officials.

Gambling must exist before there is any attempt to fix a game. In 1919, gambling was enjoying a boom period. Professional gamblers did business at every major league baseball park. If the owners saw any danger in this, they did not speak out. Some even said that it created interest in the games and helped to fill the stands.

"Players in my day bet freely," Chick Gandil, one of the key figures in the White Sox scandal once said. "They would sit in the lobbies of hotels with gamblers, gabbing away, as if nobody would ever stop them.

"I was surprised, however, when 'Sport' Sullivan [a small-time gambler] suggested we get together a syndicate of seven or eight guys to throw the series to Cincinnati. I never figured him for a fixer."

Sullivan is said to have told Gandil he would give ten thousand dollars to each player he could get to take part in the scheme. Gandil knew exactly who to contact.

At the end of June 1921, more than a year and a half after the infamous series, seven members of the White Sox and ten gamblers were brought to trial. The case against the eighth player, Fred McMullin, was dropped because of lack of evidence. The courtroom was packed each day and newspapers gave the trial the kind of coverage usually reserved for wars and natural disasters.

The district attorney opened the case by announcing that vital evidence had disappeared. Soon after, several members of his staff resigned and accepted positions defending the players.

Once he had presented what evidence he did have, the district attorney asked for jail sentences of five years and two thousand-dollar fines. The jury, however, found all defendants innocent on all charges. Some of the players were carried out of the courtroom on the shoulders of the jurors. The crowd cheered heartily.

Any feeling of joy or triumph the players might have experienced didn't last very long. The next day, Kenesaw Mountain Landis, the first commissioner of baseball, handed down *his* verdict. Said Landis: "Regardless of the verdict of the juries, no player that throws a ball game; no player that undertakes or promises to throw a baseball game; no player that sits in a conference with a bunch of crooked players and gamblers where the ways and means of throwing games are planned and discussed, and does not promptly tell his club about it, will ever play baseball."

In the years that followed, the affair was seldom discussed or written about. The players drifted into obscurity.

Chick Gandil had disappeared before the scandal came into the open, accepting an offer to play semipro baseball in Bakersfield, California. Happy Felsch and Swede Risberg joined an "outlaw league" in Montana, where big sums of money were wagered on every game. The others undoubtedly played somewhere, too.

Slugger Joe Jackson signed with the Americus team of the South Georgia League, a league outside the jurisdiction of organized baseball. He and his team were in great demand. Joe earned more money than he had as a major leaguer.

Jackson always protested that he had played no role in the fix, that he had been victimized by Charles Comiskey. Jackson's biography, *Say It Ain't So, Joe*, published in 1979, presented new evidence to confirm his innocence.

Chick Gandil outlived all but one of the Black Sox. He spent the last years of his life working as a plumber in Calistoga, California. Apparently he was able to live down his role in the fix, for when he died his family asked the local newspaper to omit his death notice. They were afraid that readers might learn of the mistake he made in his youth, and thus the dignity he had attained in later years would be tarnished.

8

Short Takes

Sports hoaxes can occur anytime, any place. They have involved every sport. Hoaxes have been carried out by well known figures and by individuals not so well known, by men, women, and teenagers. This chapter gives a rundown.

The Plainfield Ghosts

During the 1941 season, the Plainfield (New Jersey) State Teachers College made football history, of a sort. According to the sports pages of several New Jersey and New York daily newspapers, the team manhandled one opponent after another. An undefeated season loomed.

The only problem was that Plainfield Teachers College did not exist. The team was the product of the imaginative mind of Morris Newburger, a successful Wall Street stockbrocker, and a small circle of friends. Newburger created Jerry Croyden to be the school's publicity man. Newburger dreamed up a school nickname — the Lions — a head coach named Ralph (Hurry Up) Hoblitzel, an offensive attack based on the "W" formation, and a Chinese sophomore halfback named John Chung, who scored half of the team's points. Chung got pumped up by eating plates of rice at halftime.

Plainfield Teachers College overcame Chesterton and Scott in the weeks that followed. John Chung kept churning out the yardage, averaging 9.3 yards per carry. *The New York Times*, *The New York Herald Tribune*, and *The Philadelphia Record* were among the newspapers that carefully recorded Plainfield's weekly triumphs.

Toward the end of the season, Newburger became aware that someone was getting wise to his hoax. He sent out this press release: "Due to flunkings in the midterm examinations, Plainfield Teachers College has been forced to call off its last two scheduled games with Appalachian Tech tomorrow and with Harmony Teachers College on Thanksgiving Day. Among those thrown for a loss was John Chung, who has accounted for sixty-nine of Plainfield's one hundred seventeen points."

What caused Newburger to close up shop was an article under the byline of Caswell Adams that appeared in *The New York Herald Tribune*, revealing Plainfield Teachers College and John Chung as inventions of Newburger's. *Time* magazine, in its issue of November 17, also exposed the hoax. Morris Newburger and his friends went back to dealing in stocks and bonds, and Plainfield Teachers College melted away, never to be heard of again.

Phantom of the Yankees

Regarded by many experts as the greatest baseball team of all time, the 1927 New York Yankees set an American League record with one hundred ten victories in the regular season, and smashed the Pittsburgh Pirates in the World Series in four games. In every available picture of the team, a solemn-faced young man in a shirt too large for him stands in the back row between Babe Ruth and Bob Meusel. The player's name is Don Miller. He never played for the Yankees. He never played in a single major league game.

As the story goes, Miller was a minor league pitcher who was offered a tryout by the Yankees late in the season. The day the tryout was scheduled also happened to be the day the Yankees were to have their official team picture taken. As the photographer was getting the players arranged, Miller squeezed into the back row beside the Babe.

Miller flunked his tryout and never got to the big leagues. He was never heard from after that memorable day he stood amidst the Yankee heroes and had his picture taken.

Teenage Imposter

More than eighty thousand spectators packed the huge River Plate Stadium in Buenos Aires, Argentina, in January 1981 for the final match of an international soccer tournament for boys age fourteen and under. In a thrill-packed game, decided by penalty kicks following an overtime period, Internazzionale of Milan (Inter, for short), one of the richest clubs in Italy, defeated the Tahuichi Club of Bolivia. Inter forward Massimo Ottolenghi, who scored seven goals during the final matches, was named the tournament's outstanding player and awarded a handsome trophy.

The Inter boys returned to Italy in triumph. An enormous crowd of well-wishers greeted them at the Rome airport on their arrival. They appeared on television and were saluted with countless newspaper stories. At San Siro Stadium in Milan, where Inter's adult team played, the boys were introduced one by one before a First Division game match.

But Massimo Ottolenghi was not at San Siro Stadium that day. There was good reason for the boy to be absent. Early in February, *Il Manifesto*, a small daily newspaper in Milan, published an article that unsettled every Italian soccer fan. "This is the story of P., a sad boy," said the article. "In reality, P. ought to be a happy boy. He is only fourteen years old, and a few weeks ago he became a world champion.

"But he is sad because he can't tell anyone about his victory. Perhaps not even Ivanoe Fraizzoli knows the story."

Ivanoe Fraizzoli, a wealthy industrialist, was the president of the Inter club. When he read the story in *Il Manifesto*, he immediately called for an investigation. It confirmed his worst fears. Massimo Ottolenghi had never set foot in Argentina. Someone else had played in his place. That someone was Massimo Pellegrini — "P." It was Pellegrini who scored the seven goals and accepted the trophy as the outstanding player. And he had done it all under the name of Massimo Ottolenghi. The reason Pellegrini didn't qualify for the Inter team was not that he wasn't good enough — his seven goals in Milan proved his skill. Pellegrini was simply too old for the competition. He was nearly sixteen years of age.

Newspapermen tracked down Pellegrini, a shy boy, in his hometown of Frascati, just outside Rome. When was he born, he was asked. On March 23, 1966, at Frascati, he answered. But Pellegrini was not telling the truth. He was born in 1965. His mother then revealed to reporters that a team official had called the family, urging that she say nothing about her son's trip to Argentina, and she told him to keep quiet, too.

But it was too late. All of Italy soon knew of the illicit player substitution.

Eventually, Mario Fiore, secretary of Inter's youth soccer program, confessed to playing a key role in the plot, saying that he had taken Pellegrini to Argentina, knowing that he was over the age limit. Fiore explained that Pellegrini usually played on the team, and he did not think it right to change. "Besides," Fiore added, "other teams had players who were three or four years over age."

No one accepted Fiore's explanation. The Inter club suspended him and two other officials, including the team's coach.

Italian soccer had been rocked by scandal before. During the 1960s, some of Italy's most famous players had taken part in fixing games, and had been suspended as a result. While Inter's players were not involved in the fixing scandal, there were accusations that the club had once sought to bribe officials in an important European Cup match. One referee, who had clearly favored the Inter team, turned up in an exclusive resort on the Adriatic coast, vacationing at Inter's expense.

Fixing games is bad. Corrupting officials is probably worse. But the world of soccer agreed that nothing could be more shocking than involving young teenagers in crimes of deception.

Secret Weapon

In 1962, when Vince Lombardi was just beginning to achieve greatness as coach of the National Football League's Green Bay Packers, he was named to coach the Western Conference team in the annual All-Pro Game to be played the following January. The Los Angeles Coliseum was to be the site of the game.

Once the players had assembled and started practicing, Lombardi noticed that many of them were tense and fatigued following the long season. And, since the men represented many different teams, and most had never met one another, the squad lacked the spirit and comradeship a winning team must have.

Lombardi knew how to deal with these problems. His plan focused upon a big wooden crate that he had delivered to the locker room. On the outside of the crate, in large black letters, these words were printed: U.S. LINES * THIS SIDE UP * USE NO HOOKS * FOR SHIPPING PURPOSES ONLY.

One half of the crate's top surface took the form of a hinged door that was bolted shut. On one side of the crate, there was a six-inch square opening which was covered with wire mesh.

Lombardi explained to the players that the crate contained his pet mongoose. Slender and minklike in appearance, the mongoose, which is native to India, can be a ferocious animal. It is well known for its ability to kill cobras and other poisonous snakes.

Lombardi told the players they could view the mongoose through the wire mesh. "But the animal would like nothing better than a mouthful of human flesh," Lombardi warned. "Keep your fingers away from the opening."

One day, Lombardi and one of his players were together in the locker room. Their attention fell upon the crate. The player asked some questions about the mongoose and its habits.

"Take a look at him," Lombardi urged. The player peered through the wire mesh but couldn't see anything.

"Get closer," said Lombardi. "Rap on the wire. Get his attention."

As soon as the player had gotten up close to the crate and had touched the wire screen, Lombardi pushed a lever at the back of the crate. The lid sprang open. Out shot a ten-inch squirrel tail attached to an elastic band that caused it to dance up and down about a foot above the crate.

The player screamed in horror. He had no idea it was a squirrel tail. He threw himself on the floor and covered his head with his arms. Then he heard Lombardi roaring with laughter. The player soon began laughing, too.

One victim was enough to get the ball rolling. Lombardi and the player who had been tricked approached a second player and asked, "Want to see the mongoose?" After that man had been victimized, another was sought out.

Each man was frightened as badly as the first had been. The laughter got louder and louder.

Within a few days, Lombardi's plan had been executed. Every player on the squad had "seen the mongoose." They all were relaxed and uplifted in spirit.

P.S.: The Western Conference won, thirty-one to thirty.

The Wrong Page

During most of the 1940s, there was no better relief pitcher in baseball than New York Yankee left-hander Joe Page. He threw a steaming fastball and never seemed to get arm-weary. Whenever the Yankees needed him, Page was ready.

In 1947, Page won fourteen games and saved seventeen. Two years later, he had thirteen wins and twenty-seven saves. That season Allie Reynolds, the ace of the Yankee staff, won seventeen games, and ten of those were saved by Page.

By the end of the decade, however, Page's skills were fading. In 1950, he won only three of ten decisions and his earned-run-average ballooned to 5.04. That was his last year with the Yankees, his last in baseball, in fact, except for an unsuccessful comeback attempt with the Pittsburgh Pirates in 1954.

Little was heard of Joe Page in the years that

followed. He operated a restaurant in Laughing-town, Pennsylvania. Married, he lived a quiet life.

People were talking about Joe Page again in 1973. In March that year, an article in *Sport* Magazine reported: "Since his baseball career ended, Page has had little but trouble. His first marriage ended in divorce. His second wife died. He owned a bar for a while. He held a few insignificant jobs briefly.

"Now, mostly," said the article, "he drinks."

When Joe Page read the article, he became enraged. There was little truth to what the magazine said. He did not drink excessively. He had been operating, and still operated, his restaurant in Laughingtown. Mildred Page was alive and well.

Page called his lawyer and suit was filed, with the former Yankee pitcher claiming that the magazine had characterized him as a "drunkard, barfly, and a braggart." An out of court settlement was reached in February 1976.

During the pre-trial hearings, it was disclosed that Dick Schaap, the editor of *Sport* at the time, had been duped by an impostor, a man who was able to convince Shaap that he was Joe Page. Dick Schaap's article was based on what he heard from the impostor. No one ever found out who the "fake" Joe Page was or why he did it.

Indians, 1; British, 0

When Europeans first visited Canada in the 1600s, they found the Indians there playing an unusual game called *baggataway*. Members of opposing teams attempted to send a small ball across each other's goal line using a stick at the end of which was a pocket made of strips of animal hide. Because the stick looked like a bishop's cross, the French called the sport *lacrosse*, the name by which it is known today.

But modern-day lacrosse, played with ten members on a side, bears only a slight resemblance to the Indian game from which it is derived. There was always considerable ceremony associated with baggataway. Some contests were preceded by feasting and frenzied dancing. Others involved elaborate religious ceremonies. Women never participated in the games. Instead they were spectators, running up and down the sides of the field, rooting for their teams, slashing at the men with stout switches in an effort to make them play more furiously.

There was no limit to the size of opposing teams. Anyone who wanted to join in could do so. While it was usual for there to be from seventy-five to two hundred men on a side, sometimes as many as a thousand players participated.

Medicine men served as the game's officials. The goal lines were marked by the spot where rival medicine men stood. If one of them decided to take a short hike, the goal line moved along with him. Sometimes the line shifted as much as five or ten miles in one direction or another during the course of a game.

A game of baggataway was once used to trick a large force of British troops and helped to trigger one of the worst massacres in Canadian history. Two Indian tribes, the Chippewas and the Sacs, were responsible for the plot. The Chippewas lived in a region of Canada where Fort Michillmackinac — now Fort Mackinac — in the province of Ontario was located.

One spring day in 1763, a time when the British were tightening their grip on their Canadian empire, the Sacs sent a large delegation to visit the Chippewas. They arrived just before June 4, the birth date of George III, a British holiday. The Chippewas sent word to the commander of the fort that they would like to play a game of baggataway in honor of the king's birthday, with a team representing the Chippewas opposing a Sac team. Soldiers occupying the fort and the traders and trappers staying there were invited to attend the match.

The commander of the fort was suspicious, believing that the Indians might be baiting a trap. He replied that his men would not leave the fort. That didn't seem to bother the Indians. They said that they would play the game close to the fort so that those inside could watch through the openings in the fort walls and the gun parapets.

On the appointed day, the game got underway early in the morning in a field near the fort. Little by little, soldiers and others inside the fort began to drift out through the fort gates to stand and watch the contest from the sidelines. Some spectators sprawled on the ground. The fort gates remained open.

Throngs of Indian women were seated along the sidelines nearest to the fort. All had heavy blankets draped about their shoulders, even though the day grew warm.

Suddenly, one of the players tossed the ball toward the fort gate. That was the signal. The other Indians dropped their sticks and ran toward the women at the sideline who passed them tomahawks and other weapons from beneath their blankets. Then the men rushed into the fort.

According to one account, there were only three survivors. One of them, Alexander Henry, who was captured and carried away, later managed to escape. He told the story of the massacre in a book he wrote titled, *Travels and Adventures in Canada and the Indian Territories.*

Today, lacrosse is staple among spring sports in the eastern United States, and a growing favorite elsewhere in the country. It is played by thousands of club teams, high schools, and colleges. Women participate on every level. The tragic chapter in the sport's history recounted here has all but been forgotten.

Football Trickery

During the first decades of the present century, the Carlisle Indians were one of the most successful teams in college football. Representing the Carlisle Indian School in Carlisle, Pennsylvania, the team was coached by Glenn S. (Pop) Warner, one of football's first tactical wizards.

Coach Warner had only a handful of boys of football age to draw upon in building the Carlisle team. As a result, there was usually a shortage of substitutes for Carlisle games. The Indians were also at a disadvantage because many of them were small in stature. "I never had a team that averaged over one hundred seventy pounds," Warner once said.

The Carlisle team was successful because the players were well coached and had tremendous enthusiasm, tearing heavier lines to pieces and tackling with great fury. They also relied on trick plays. "They were what the Indians loved best," Warner once said. "There was never a time when they wouldn't rather have won by an eyelash and a trick play, than by a large score with straight football."

The Indians' greatest joy was in executing the hidden ball trick. Warner first called upon the play in a game against Harvard in 1903.

The Harvard team kicked off and the ball sailed high and far down the field to be gathered in by Jimmy Johnson on the five-yard line. The Indian players converged upon Johnson, forming a huddle around him. Thus concealed, Johnson slipped the ball under the back of Charlie Dillon's jersey. Dillon had been picked for the assignment because he was six-feet tall and could run very fast. In addition, Dillon was a guard and was less likely to be suspected of carrying the ball.

"Go!" yelled Johnson when the ball was in place. The Carlisle players fanned out toward the sidelines. Each backfield man removed his helmet and clutched it to his chest, as if carrying a football. While the Harvard tacklers were pursuing the Carlisle backfield men, Dillon charged straight down the field for the Harvard goal line. Since he had his hands free, no one suspected that he had the ball. In fact, the Harvard safety man, the last player between Dillon and the goal, thought the

Indian runner was going to block him, so he side-stepped to let Dillon go by.

The spectators laughed and cheered. Most of them were able to see Dillon's bulged-out back and were aware of what was happening. When Dillon crossed the goal line, one of his teammates jerked out the ball and touched it to the ground. An official signaled a touchdown had been scored.

Unhappily, the hidden ball trick was not enough to win the game for Carlisle. Harvard scored two touchdowns against the outmanned Indians in the second half to gain a one-point victory.

In 1908, when Carlisle faced Harvard another time, Warner had a new trick to try. Before the game, he had brown, oval-shaped patches sewn on his players' jerseys and pants. Being the same color and size as a football, the pads made it difficult to tell which players actually had the ball.

Percy Haughton, the Harvard coach, went to Warner and complained. "That's not fair," said Haughton.

"It's not against the rules," grinned Warner. "I can put anything I like on my players' jerseys."

But Haughton had a trick of his own to unveil. Just before the kickoff, he and Warner met at the center of the field to choose the game football. As the home team, it was Harvard's responsibility to provide the ball. Haughton carried out a bag of footballs, opened it, and invited Warner to select one. Warner reached in and picked out one. A look of astonishment crossed his face. The ball was bright red, the same color as the Harvard jerseys. Warner realized immediately the confusion the red ball would cause. He reached in for another ball. It was red, too. He peered into the bag. All the footballs were red.

"It's not against the rules," Haughton said, a wide smile on his face. "A football doesn't have to be *brown*, does it?"

Warner walked back to the Carlisle bench muttering to himself. Harvard won the game, seventeen to zero.

Blitzing the Bookmakers

Elaborate hoaxes have also been used to pull off betting swindles. One of the most famous occurred in London over the Easter weekend of 1780. The scheme depended on the fact that the Easter weekend represents the height of the racing season in England. Holiday meetings are scheduled in every part of the country.

The fixers launched their scheme by sending a letter to the editor of a leading racing newspaper of the day called *The Sporting Life*. The letter, a most courteous one, was supposedly written by the secretary of the Trodmore Hunt, a race meeting to be held on Easter Monday.

With the letter, the writer enclosed a list of the horses and riders that would be participating in the meet. "After the meet," the letter declared, "I will be sending you the results by telegram."

The editor of *The Sporting Life* welcomed the letter. It meant relief for his overworked staff. He was happy to print the list of horses and riders enclosed with the letter.

The next day, the editor received the telegram.

Without the slightest hesitation, he printed the information it contained. People all over London placed bets on the race — bets that were based solely on the information in the letter. London bookmakers paid out several thousand pounds to customers who had been extremely lucky with their bets on the Trodmore races.

No one might have realized that a swindle had taken place had not a second racing paper reprinted the Trodmore results as they appeared in *The Sporting Life*. But a misprint occurred. The second paper listed as seven to two the price paid by a winning horse (meaning that a two-pound bet would have returned seven pounds in winnings). In *The Sporting Life*, the price was listed at five to two.

The secretary of the Trodmore Hunt had to be contacted to establish which price was correct. This was difficult to do. There was no secretary. There was no Trodmore Hunt. Indeed, in all of England there was no such a place as Trodmore.

Fiasco in the Ring

Jake LaMotta, a well known boxer of the late 1940s and early 1950s, had a simple strategy: wade in and throw punches. A motion picture based on his life, released in 1981, has an appropriate name. It was called *Raging Bull*.

But in at least one of his bouts, LaMotta did not rage. He was relaxed and calm, so relaxed and calm, in fact, that whispers that the fight was fixed began to be heard almost from the moment the two fighters answered the opening bell.

The bout in question took place in November 1947 at New York's Madison Square Garden. LaMotta's opponent that night was Billy Fox, a Philadelphia light-heavyweight with a reputation as a good puncher. He had won forty-nine of fifty fights.

LaMotta, besides his raging-bull qualities, was also known as a fighter who could take it. He had battled the best fighters in his weight class, and, although he didn't always win, he had never been knocked out in his long career.

In his bout against Billy Fox, LaMotta started fast but faded quickly. He kept leaving his chin unguarded. Fox wasted no time in finding it. In the second round, one of Fox's blows sent La Motta reeling against the ropes.

The third round was fairly even but the fourth was all Fox's. He rushed across the ring and staggered LaMotta with a powerful left hook to the chin. Jake rocked back on his heels. But instead of trying to defend himself, LaMotta let his hands fall to his sides. Fox moved in, pounding LaMotta with his fists. LaMotta took every punch.

After the referee had separated the two fighters, Fox went after LaMotta again, hitting him with every kind of punch he knew how to throw. The referee separated the fighters again. Fox moved in one more time, pounding away at LaMotta's head.

At this point, the referee stepped in and stopped the bout, awarding the victory to Fox. The crowd filled the arena with loud boos. Cries of "Fix! Fix! Fix!" rained down on the fighters.

State boxing officials called for investigation. Both fighter's purses were held up.

LaMotta and several others were questioned. LaMotta defended his poor showing by claiming he was injured. Approximately a month before the fight with Billy Fox, LaMotta said, he had suffered painful damage to his spleen during a training session. Boxing officials then suspended LaMotta for concealing information concerning his physical condition.

Insiders laughed at this decision. There was talk that LaMotta had allowed Fox to win on orders from the criminal element that controlled boxing at the time.

Little was heard of Billy Fox following his victory over LaMotta. LaMotta, however, became the world's middleweight champion two years later. But his feeble performance against Billy Fox was never forgotten, and is looked upon with greater suspicion than any other bout in modern ring history.

Con Man

His real name was Alvin Clarence Thomas, but during the 1920s, he was known far and wide as Titanic Thompson. Among the world's bunco artists, or swindlers, Titanic had few equals. He was original and imaginative, never without a trick up his sleeve.

Whenever Titanic made a bet, he seldom left the results to chance. One day, Titanic was driving into Omaha with a friend. They passed a highway sign announcing that they were ten miles from the city limits. Titanic looked at his watch. "We should be there in ten minutes," he announced. His friend bet they wouldn't. He had no way of knowing that Titanic had moved the sign post five miles closer to the city that morning.

Titanic often boasted of owning a magnificent throwing arm, developed, he said, by hunting quail with rocks during his boyhood in Arkansas. He once bet a doubter that he could throw a pumpkin over a three-story tenement building. On the day the wager was to be decided, Titanic showed up with a pumpkin the size of an orange. He won the bet with ease.

Golf was Titanic's game. He was once matched against an amateur player who could drive the ball out of sight. Since the long hitter wasn't always accurate, hitting to the left sometimes, to the right other times, Titanic offered to let him hit three drives on each hole, and play the best one.

The amateur took a comfortable lead in the early stages of the match. Titanic didn't seem troubled. By the halfway point, the amateur's arms began to tire from taking three full swings on each hole. In the final stages, he hardly had enough strength to lift his driver out of the bag. Titanic overtook him on the sixteenth hole and won by a big margin.

Another time, Titanic lost twenty-five hundred dollars in a dice game and decided to use golf to get his money back, betting his opponent he could drive a ball five hundred yards. Even the most powerful hitters in professional golf seldom drive as much as three hundred fifty yards. "And you can furnish the ball," said Titanic.

On a freezing cold winter day, Titanic and his

friend drove to a golf course on New York's Long Island. Titanic picked out an elevated tee that overlooked a big lake. The lake was frozen solid. Titanic teed up the ball and took a mighty swing. The ball traveled about one hundred seventy-five yards in the air, hit down on the ice, then kept bouncing until it was in the next zip code and beyond.

Titanic would always find a way to win. He once opposed Nick the Greek Dandolus in a game of golf. On the final hole, Nick had a twenty-five foot putt. Titanic bet him ten thousand dollars that he couldn't run it in. Nick the Greek stepped up to the ball and holed it.

Titanic's expression never changed. He simply offered to bet Nick double or nothing that he could hit a silver dollar eight times in eight shots with a pistol at a range of fifteen feet. "You're on!" said Nick, feeling the feat was impossible. But Titanic did it, saving his ten thousand dollars. He tossed the coin to Nick as a souvenir.

Shocker

It would take a book the size of this one to describe all of the methods crooked owners, trainers, and jockeys have used to speed up (or slow down) horses in an effort to control the outcome of a race. Various watchdog agencies, such as the New York Racing Association, seek to prevent fixed races from ever happening, but the crooks never stop trying.

One of the simplest and most frequently used methods of getting a horse to run faster is the electric prod. About the size of a pocket lighter, the prod consists of a penlight battery with two small rods at each end. When a button is pressed, a current flows through the rods, creating an electric shock to make the horse run faster.

Sometimes such a device will also give off a buzzing sound when the button is pressed. The horse must be trained to respond to the buzzer.

Since the electric prod is so small, it is easy for a jockey to conceal it in his clothing or his hand. At the start of a race, or at some other critical moment, the jockey sets off the charge.

At Belmont Park in New York on the afternoon of June 22, 1981, Dr. Manuel Gilman, a veterinarian employed by the New York Racing Association, was watching the horses being put into the starting gate for the second race. About half of the horses had been locked in the gate when Dr. Gilman saw an object tossed from the gate area. After the start of the race, he picked up the object and examined it. It was an electric prod.

An investigation followed. Jockeys, trainers, the race starter, assistant starters, and pony boys were questioned. As a result of the investigation, it was determined that the battery had been in the possession of Larry Saumell, a thirty-four-year-old jockey from Wheeling, West Virginia. Saumell rode a horse named Jack's Pet in the race.

Saumell was immediately barred from riding at all race tracks under the jurisdiction of the New York Racing Association. "Once we know someone is guilty of something," said a security official, "we won't permit them to take part in the races. It's not fair to the betting public."

Only a month before the Saumell incident, a similar incident occurred at Arlington Park in Chicago. Jockey Ben Feliciano was barred for five years for possessing a battery.

Saumell, at five-foot-six, was tall for a jockey. He had been riding professionally for eight years and had ridden exactly nine hundred winners.

In the race in question, Saumell's mount, Jack's Pet, finished dead last. Obviously, the horse needed help. But not a battery.

Marathon Hoaxers

For well over a decade, women long-distance runners ran not only for their health and the sense of achievement they derived from their sport, but also for equality with men. Women were barred from competing in marathons until fairly recent times. This was because of the widespread belief that women were not capable of running the distance of a marathon (over twenty-six miles).

"I was called a weirdo," says Nina Kuscsik, a pioneer in women's marathoning. "I was made to feel different, just because I was trying to improve my body."

Women had to resort to trickery to convince officials that they were capable of running the marathon distance. Take what happened in 1966, for example. That year, Roberta Gibb, a young woman from Winchester, Massachusetts, made up her mind to participate in the Boston Marathon, the oldest and the most renowned long distance event in the United States. But Boston officials had never permitted a woman to run in their race. They would make no exception for Roberta Gibb, even though she was a capable distance performer and had trained hard. Her entry form was rejected by race officials.

On the day of the race, Roberta decided to run anyway. Just before the race began, she hid in a clump of bushes not far from the starting line. She could see the starter as he raised his pistol. She heard the gun go off. When the runners went pounding past her, Roberta jumped into the pack.

Roberta was wearing a hooded sweatshirt and baggy sweat pants, clothing that disguised the fact she was a woman. But as the day grew warmer, she shed her outer clothing, and sped along in a leotard and a pair of shorts.

Roberta completed the race in a time of three hours, twenty-one minutes, two seconds, a fine performance. She finished one hundred twenty fourth in a field of four hundred sixteen.

Afterward, marathon officials refused to admit that Roberta had taken part in the race. "I know of no woman who ran," said Will Cloney, the director of the event. "Our rules do not permit women to run."

The next year, 1967, women exerted more pressure. Race officials received an entry blank from one "K. Switzer," and accepted it. The K could have stood for Karl or Ken. But it did not. The K was for Kathy. Kathy Switzer was a nineteen-year-old sophomore at Syracuse University, an enthusiastic runner.

On race day, Kathy's male coach went to the school gym in Hopkinton, Massachusetts, where the runners assembled before the race, and picked up her official number. It was a chilly day and a light drizzle was falling. Kathy donned layers of bulky clothing to keep warm.

At the starting line, Kathy had no trouble mixing in with the other runners. Because she was wearing an official number, no one questioned her. The race began without incident.

But after she had traveled a mile or so, Kathy removed the hood of the sweatshirt she was wearing. Newspaper reporters in a bus following the runners suddenly realized that a woman was running in the Boston Marathon. Sports history was being made.

Jock Semple, one of the race directors, was furious. He darted out onto the course and began pursuing Kathy. "I'm going to get you out of the race!" he shouted. "I'm going to get you out!"

As Semple caught up with her, he tried to rip the number off of Kathy's running suit. Suddenly, Kathy's boyfriend, Tom Miller, who was running with her, charged into Semple, hitting him with a powerful shoulder block. Semple went sprawling.

"The rest of the race was agony for me," Kathy was to say afterward. "Tom hit Semple hard, very hard. Everytime we got to a corner and I'd see a cop standing there, I expected him to step out and arrest us."

Kathy finished the race in four hours, twenty minutes, about two hours behind the winner. Not long after, the Amateur Athletic Union (A.A.U.)

banned Kathy and other women from competing with men.

But the women fought back. The picture of Kathy being shoved around by Jock Semple became a rallying point for women fighting discrimination in sports.

In 1972, the A.A.U. reversed its position, and approved marathon running for men and women in the same race. That same year, women were permitted to run officially in the Boston Marathon for the first time.

By the late 1970s, women were welcomed in marathons everywhere, and early in 1980 Olympic officials announced that there would be a marathon for women in the Olympic Games in 1984. Previously, Olympic officials had always ignored women marathoners. A little trickery had paid big dividends.

9

The Great American Baseball Hoax

On a warm, sunshiny morning in 1839, Abner Doubleday, a student at Green's Select School in Cooperstown, New York, called some of his friends together in an open field where they usually played the old English schoolboy game of rounders.

Doubleday was excited. He had written up the rules for a ball-and-stick game somewhat similar to rounders, and he was eager to see how they were going to be received. He had laid out a playing field, a "diamond," as he called it, with three bases and a home plate.

There were to be nine men to a side. Since Doubleday had observed that it took about ninety feet for a man to achieve top running speed, he placed the bases ninety feet apart. The pitcher was to stand sixty feet, six inches from home plate.

Doubleday and his friends chose up sides and the game began. Apple pie had already been invented. The hot dog would come later. But now America had baseball.

The only trouble with this story is that it never happened. It is a pleasant myth, but it's only a myth. And like most myths, this one has gained wide acceptance.

There is no doubt that Abner Doubleday was an important man in his time. After Green's Select School, he attended West Point. He later rose to the rank of brigadier general in the U.S. Army. He was a member of the Federal garrison at Fort Sumter in 1861 when Confederate forces fired upon the fort, an event that signaled the outbreak of the Civil War. Doubleday, an artillery captain, sighted the first field gun fired on the Union side.

Doubleday wrote detailed accounts of the battles of Chancellorsville and Gettysburg, where he commanded the Union Army at the close of the first day of fighting. Later, while on duty at a military base in San Francisco, Doubleday suggested the first cable-operated streetcar in America, and obtained a charter for its construction. San Francisco's cable cars, of course, are one of the city's chief attractions today. Doubleday died in Mendham, New Jersey, in 1893.

Doubleday went many places and did many things. But there is not the slightest bit of evidence that he invented the game of baseball. He probably never even played the game.

There is, in fact, a tall stack of evidence that indicates that Doubleday had nothing to do with baseball. He was a man who kept a careful account of his life and times. When he died, his heirs came into possession of the sixty-seven diaries in which Doubleday set down a lifetime of experiences and observations. Not one of the volumes mentioned baseball.

In the years following the Civil War, when baseball was first being offered as professional entertainment, the General made no reference to the sport in his writings. By the time Doubleday died in 1893, baseball had attained a good measure of popularity. Surely a person that had invented the game would have come forth to take a few bows. But Abner Doubleday said nothing, strange conduct for a man who would be named "the father of the game."

As for Cooperstown, New York, there is no reason to honor the town as the birthplace of the sport. True, organized baseball has seen fit to establish a museum and hall of fame in Cooperstown, which are visited by many thousands of people each year. But it is not likely that the people of Cooperstown ever knew what baseball looked like until the 1860s or later.

To understand how The Great American Baseball Hoax developed, let's go back to the years 1934 and 1935. Interest in baseball was sagging. Club owners began searching around for an idea that would heighten the game's appeal.

Someone offered the owners a report on the origins of baseball that had been prepared by A.G. Mills in 1907. Although it was covered with a few decades of dust, baseball officials seized upon the report as if it were heaven-sent.

The report named young Abner Doubleday of Cooperstown, New York, as the game's founder. It fixed 1839 as the year that Doubleday had invented the sport. This fact offered special appeal to the owners. It would enable them to beat the drums for baseball's one hundredth birthday, in 1939, which was just a few years away.

Soon after, plans for the centennial were announced. Funds were raised to build an official hall of fame at Cooperstown. Week after week, newspapers supported the planned festivities with articles and photographs.

So it was that on June 11, 1939, there were parades, speeches, and dedications at Cooperstown. There was a "comeback" by Babe Ruth, who had retired in 1935, and the re-creation of a baseball game played according to the rules supposedly written by Abner Doubleday in 1839.

Baseball commissioner Kenesaw Mountain Landis dedicated the newly erected Hall of Fame "to all Americans." Also dedicated was Doubleday Field, said to have been built on the actual spot where Doubleday's pioneers had trotted into action exactly one hundred years before.

Ten members of the Hall of Fame were presented with engraved bats. The ruffle of drums and the playing of taps answered the calling of the names of the fourteen deceased Hall of Famers.

What's troublesome about all of this is that no one had ever taken the trouble to study the report that had been prepared by A.G. Mills upon which all the hoopla was based. If the Mills report had been investigated, it would have been found to contain about as much factual information as *The Wizard of Oz*.

How did the Mills report come into existence?

Its origins went back to the turn of the century. A.G. Spalding, who had been a pitcher, manager, and an owner, a towering figure in the early days of the game, became curious as to how baseball began.

The editor of Spalding's *Baseball Guide*, Henry Chadwick, told him that the sport was of foreign ancestry. Chadwick pointed out that the French played a game in the 12th century with milking stools as bases. The ancient Egyptians had a sacred stick-and-ball game that could be taken as a distant cousin to baseball.

Chadwick also informed Spalding that there was a direct link between baseball and the English game of rounders. Played on a field similar in size to a softball field, and with nine players on a side, rounders offered tall posts as bases and had a pitcher — called a bowler — who threw underhand to the batter. Chadwick was of English birth and had been a rounders player.

Spalding felt that Chadwick was biased toward the English. A series of friendly arguments followed.

Or perhaps they weren't so friendly. Spalding was a man who was used to having his own way. He owned and operated the nation's first sporting goods company (a firm that bears his name to this day). He suffered only one known disappointment in his life, when he ran for the U.S. Senate and was defeated.

"I claim," Spalding said, "baseball owes its prestige as our National Game to the fact that no other form of the sport is such an exponent of American courage, confidence, combativeness, dash, discipline, determination, energy, eagerness, pluck, persistency, performance spirit, sagacity, success, vim, vigor, and virility."

Spalding said more. "It would be impossible," he declared, "for a Briton, who had not breathed the air of this free land as a naturalized American citizen . . . to play baseball." It would be just as unlikely for an American, he claimed, to play the national games of England.

Chadwick, however, offered serious opposition to what Spalding said. He had been a baseball observer since the 1840s, had devised the baseball boxscore, and had been one of the first writers to offer reports and comments on the game. He, too, as in the case of Doubleday and a couple of others, would be called the "Father of Baseball."

Spalding suggested, in 1905, that a committee be formed to investigate how baseball had originated. Spalding promised that he would accept the committee's finding. And why not? The individuals who made up the committees were all members of baseball's founding brotherhood. They were about as likely to call baseball an English game as they were to suggest that Theodore Roosevelt, the President of the United States at the time, was of Oriental heritage.

The committee included:

• A.G. Mills of New York, the third president of the National League. Named committee chairman, it was Mills who, in 1880, created the reserve clause, which bound a player for life to the first team with which he signed (and which served as the focal point of the baseball players' strike in 1981).

- Morgan G. Bulkeley of Hartford, Connecticut, who had been the first president of the National League. Later he served as governor of Connecticut and a U.S. Senator.

- Arthur P. Gorman of Maryland, a baseball player in the 1850s and 1860s, who also was to become a U.S. Senator.

- Nicholas E. Young of Washington, D.C., who had been a baseball player as a young man and later served as president of the National League.

- Al Reach of Philadelphia, another early-day ball player and a sporting goods manufacturer.

- George Wright, one of the first baseball stars.

- James E. Sullivan, president of the A.A.U. (Amateur Athletic Union).

Most of the members of the committee did not look seriously upon the task that confronted them. The matter, they felt, was simply part of the long dispute between Spalding and Chadwick. They were busy men; they had other things to do.

A year passed without any report being issued by the committee. Spalding grew impatient. He put pressure on Mills to speed up the investigation and prepare a report.

As the pressure was mounting, Mills received a letter from Abner Graves, an eighty-nine-year-old retired mining engineer from Denver. Graves claimed that he was there that day in Cooperstown when Abner Doubleday invented baseball. His memory had not become clouded despite the passage of sixty-eight years. He said he could recall the day down to the tiniest detail.

"Doubleday laid down the baseball rules, much as they are today," Graves said in his letter. "The game has not changed much since that time."

The letter from Graves pleased Mills, who had known Doubleday quite well. They had fought together in Gettysburg and had kept in touch with one another through the years. Now, Mills had the opportunity to honor an old friend, dead some fourteen years, and at the same time give Spalding the red-blooded American folk hero he was seeking.

Mills presented his report on December 30, 1907. It was more in the nature of a personal letter than a statement of committee findings, because all the other members of the committee avoided signing it.

"In the days when Abner Doubleday attended school in Cooperstown," Mills began, "it was common for two dozen or more schoolboys to join him in a game of ball. It is easy to understand how this West Point graduate would devise a scheme for limiting the contestants on each side and allotting to them field positions, each with a certain amount of territory, also substituting the existing method of putting out the base runner for the old one of plugging him with the ball."

From beginning to end, Mills's report was filled with inaccuracies. Doubleday, in 1839, was twenty years old, and was not attending school in Cooperstown. Instead, he was in his second year as a West Point cadet.

The practice of "plugging," which Mills said Doubleday had put an end to, continued as a feature of the game for many years after 1839. To "plug" a runner was to put him out by throwing the ball at him, aiming at his ribs or backside. It was also called "burning" or "scorching."

Mills also credited Doubleday with making a diagram of the baseball diamond. But he offered no copy of the diagram and none is known to have existed. Until Mills issued his report in 1907, the town of Cooperstown was as unaware that anyone named Doubleday ever played baseball there.

It is also interesting to note that neither Spalding or Chadwick, both of whom were closely connected with the game, had ever heard of Doubleday. It was also news to them that baseball was founded in the year 1839 in Cooperstown. Spalding, who started playing the game in the 1860s, remained closely associated with it until his death in 1915. Chadwick, who died in 1908, was a student of baseball for more than sixty years.

Spalding accepted Mills's report and carefully stored it away. But not before he had it reprinted in his book, *The National Game*, published in 1910. A copy of the book made its way into the hands of the committee of baseball executives, and served as the basis for the plans they developed to honor the date they designated as baseball's one hundredth birthday in 1939.

The tale of Abner Doubleday might have been believed were it not for Robert W. Henderson, a

New York librarian. Searching through West Point records, Henderson found out that Cadet Doubleday, who graduated in 1842, had not gone home to Cooperstown in the spring or summer of 1839 or any other time that year.

The attempt to cover up baseball's true origins, or at least withhold information concerning them, did no honor to A.G. Mills, A.G. Spalding, or the baseball powers of the 1930s. About the only one to come out of the affair with his reputation intact was Abner Doubleday. After all, he never said he invented baseball.

How did baseball really begin? Nobody knows for certain.

One of the essential features of the game, hitting a ball with a stick, is not something one really "invents." It is not particularly clever or unusual. It requires no great technical skill or intricate equipment. It could have been made the basis of a game at about anytime in history.

Most sources agree that baseball was derived from two other stick-and-ball games that preceded it, cricket and rounders. Cricket is a game played on a large field by two teams of eleven members each. The field is equipped with two narrow wooden frames, each twenty-eight inches in height, called wickets. The wickets are placed twenty-two yards apart.

The object of the game is to score runs. To score one run, the batter must hit the pitched ball far enough to enable him to run to the wicket opposite him before the opposition recovers the ball.

Cricket was introduced to colonial America in 1751. The colonists were busy people. They had land to clear, homes to build, and farms to tend. But there were those among them who found time for cricket, using equipment brought from England.

Young people of the 1800s are said to have preferred rounders to cricket. Rounders did not require wickets. You could make a ball by wrapping rags around a stone or piece of lead. You could cut a stick from the branch of a tree and make a bat out of it.

As the game increased in popularity, the rules were constantly improved upon. Rounders called for the use of tall stakes as bases. But since runners undoubtedly stumbled over the stakes, it made more sense to replace them with flat stones or use tree stumps. One boy would whack the ball and scamper for the base, while ten, fifteen, or even twenty others would scramble for the ball and try to plug him before he reached the safety of the base.

By the 1830s, the game was being played in several cities along the Atlantic seaboard under a variety of names. It was known as "Town Ball" in Boston and Philadelphia. It was called "One Old Cat" or "Two Old Cat" in New York. No one knows for sure when the term "base ball" (two words) was first used.

Teams in New York decided about 1841 that more and better rules were needed. This led to the sketching of the first known "Base Ball Diagram," which came into use in 1842.

By now, "base ball" was not merely a game for teenage boys; it was played by adults as well. The Knickerbocker Baseball Club of New York, which came into existence in 1845, was the first organization of its kind in history.

The Knickerbockers formed a committee to develop standard rules. A draftsman named Alexander Cartwright headed the committee.

It was Cartwright's idea to place the bases ninety feet apart, the distance that separates them today. He also suggested that to retire a man, the ball be thrown to a defensive baseman rather than *at* the runner.

Cartwright decided to put his rules to the test one Sunday morning in June 1845. A number of young men of Manhattan gathered at a grassy field about half a mile to the south and east of the reservoir, or at what is now the corner of Lexington Avenue and 34th Street. There they played one of the early variations of rounders.

Two teams were engaged in play when Cartwright interrupted, trotting out onto the field. He was holding a sheaf of papers. Cartwright stood six-foot-two, walked rod straight, and had handsome chin whiskers, so he was not easy to ignore.

Cartwright began by offering a simple diagram that showed where the bases were to be located. The players gathered in a circle as he drew the diagram in the dirt. Then, with Cartwright directing, they took positions on the field.

Cartwright explained that when a ball was batted into the field and knocked down by a defensive player, the defensive man had to throw the ball to first base in order to retire the runner. He also limited each side's turn at bat to three outs.

Most people were enthusiastic about Cartwright's rule changes, but there were some complaints. Cartwright decreed that there were to be nine men to a side. Thus, after eighteen players had been chosen, those remaining had to be satisfied being spectators. This was a new departure. Previously, everyone available got into the game.

In the days that followed, improvements were made. Canvas sacks were put down as bases. The pitcher was placed forty-five feet from home plate. (In 1881, the distance was increased to fifty feet. In 1893, it became sixty feet. When a surveyor misread "60 f." as "60-6," he established the pitching distance at sixty feet, six inches, the distance it is today.)

Today, a bronze plaque near the entrance of a 7-Eleven store at Lexington Avenue and 34th Street in Manhattan commemorates Cartwright's early efforts. The plaque reads:

ON THIS SITE
IN JUNE 1845
ALEXANDER CARTWRIGHT
ORGANIZED
THE FIRST BASEBALL GAME
PLAYED IN AMERICA UNDER
MOST OF THE RULES WHICH
GOVERN THE SPORT TODAY

On September 23, 1845, Cartwright published these rules:

1. Bases shall be from home to second, and

first to third, forty-two paces equidistant. [A pace was three feet, making the distance from home to second one hundred twenty-six feet. Presently, the distance is 127 feet, 3½ inches].

2. The game is to consist of twenty-one counts or aces, but at the conclusion and equal number of hands must be played. [An ace meant a run; a hand was an out.]

3. The ball must be pitched, not thrown for the bat. [This meant the pitcher had to use an underhand delivery.]

4. A ball knocked outside the range of first or third is foul.

5. Three balls being struck at and missed, and the last one caught is a hand out; if not caught, is considered fair and the striker bound to run.

6. A ball being struck or tipped, and caught either flying or on the first bound, is a hand out.

7. A player running the bases shall be out if the ball is in the hands of an adversary on the base and the runner is touched by it before he makes his base; it being understood, however, that in no instance is a ball to be thrown at him. [No more plugging, in other words.]

8. A player running, who shall prevent an adversary from catching or getting the ball before making his base, is a hand out.

9. Three hands out, all out.

10. No ace or base can be made on a foul strike.

11. One base allowed when the ball bounds out of the field when struck.

The next spring, the Knickerbocker Club crossed the Hudson River to Hoboken, New Jersey, and there, on a lot called Elysian Fields, faced a team that called itself the New York Nine. The Knickerbockers lost, twenty-three to one. The date was June 19, 1846. A plaque at where the field was once located reads: "It is generally considered that until this time the game [baseball] was not seriously regarded."

The Knickerbocker rules, as they were called in some quarters, did not take the country by storm. Some players felt they made baseball too gentle a game. Plugging the base runner was still favored by some teams well into the twentieth century. During a game in 1905, in a season in which he won twenty-six games in the American League, left-hander Rube Waddell pegged the ball at a runner going to second base. "That's an out where I come from," he explained.

In the latter half of the nineteenth century, Cartwright's rules were amended from time to time. For example, a rule was introduced in 1857 stating that a game was to be decided by nine innings of play (not on the basis of the first team to score twenty-one runs). There were additions, too, such as the introduction of the called strike in 1858. But if you've played baseball or seen a game, you know that most of the rules set down by Cartwright are in force today.

In 1938, when organized baseball's plans to honor Doubleday and Cooperstown were moving into high gear, they came to the attention of Bruce Cartwright, a grandson of Alexander Cartwright's. He was shocked by what he read. Abner Doubleday — who was he? Bruce Cartwright had old newspaper clippings and his grandfather's diary to prove that Alexander Cartwright was the real founder of modern baseball.

There were many red faces when Bruce Cartwright presented his evidence to baseball officials. But it did not change their plans to celebrate the one-hundredth anniversary of the game in 1939. There could be no turning back. As a compromise, baseball officials announced that there would be an "Alexander Cartwright Day" during the birthday festivities.

How much better it would have been if Spalding, Mills, and the baseball powers of the 1930s had settled upon Cartwright as the inventor of the game. Of course, that would have meant postponing baseball's one-hundredth birthday party for six years, from 1939 to 1945.

Abner Doubleday would be remembered today only as a capable Civil War general. Baseball's Hall of Fame would be located in New York City. And Cooperstown would be a sleepy little community, no better know than Middlefield or Elk Creek, or other such towns of upper New York state.

10

Scandals in Basketball

Henry Hill's life of crime touched every base. Over the years, he was connected with cases involving drugs, extortion, gambling, and the illegal transportation of untaxed cigarettes. Thirty-seven years old, from Rockville Centre, Long Island (where he lived around the corner from the police station), Hill was also a key figure in planning the theft of cash and jewels worth over five million dollars from a cargo terminal at Kennedy Airport in New York on December 11, 1978, the largest cash robbery in history.

That's not all. Henry Hill was a basketball fixer. He bribed college players to rig the outcome of basketball games. During the 1978-79 season, Hill, according to an article he wrote for *Sports Illustrated*, paid three Boston College players to shave points in nine games.

The players, said Hill, were Rick Kuhn and Jim Sweeney, who were involved from the first, and Ernie Cobb, who was recruited for the last five games. It cost Hill two thousand five hundred dollars per player per game. He won on six of the games and lost on three. He estimated that his winnings came to about one hundred thousand dollars. Seldom has hoaxing been so profitable.

Henry Hill's basketball caper had its beginnings in 1976 when Hill was serving time in Lewisburg (Pennsylvania) federal prison. While there, Hill met Paul Mazzei, a thirty-seven-year-old dog groomer from Pittsburgh who had been sentenced on a drug charge. The two became friends.

After they were released from prison, Mazzei introduced Hill to Tony Perla, who told him he had a friend named Rick Kuhn who was a basketball player at Boston College. "The kid wants to do business," Perla told Hill, according to his article in *Sports Illustrated.*

A few months later, Hill, Mazzei, Tony Perla, and Tony's brother Rocca, who had been a high school classmate of Kuhn's, began seriously discussing the fixing of games. Hill's role, to use his own words, was to be the "muscle guy," the individual who would arrange for the money and solve any problems that might arise. Hill got the approval of his bosses. Other discussions followed.

Early in December 1978, in a motel room at Logan International Airport in Boston, Hill met Kuhn and another Boston College player, Jim Sweeney, for the first time. Kuhn, twenty-five years old, six-foot-five, was a former high school star at Swissvale Area High, near Pittsburgh. At Boston College, Kuhn played three seasons, from 1976 to 1978, and was noted for his rebounding ability.

Sweeney, twenty-three years old, five feet eleven and a half inches tall, was Boston's leading player in assists, and was the only player on any Boston College team to ever be named captain three times. "He never, ever did anything wrong," a teammate once said of him. "In fact, we would make fun of him because he was such a goody-good."

Hill described the meeting as a "get acquainted session." Later in December, they met again and talked seriously. That meeting was held at the Sheraton Hotel at the Prudential Center in Boston. ". . . Kuhn and Sweeney knew exactly what I was there for," Hill wrote in *Sports Illustrated*. Kuhn wanted to be paid thirty-five hundred dollars a game, but Hill was able to convince him to accept twenty-five hundred dollars. When they started to discuss which games they would rig, Sweeney took out a copy of the Boston College schedule. He circled several games and handed the schedule to Hill.

One reason that basketball is attractive to fixers has to do with the system used in betting on the game. The person placing a bet has to do more than pick the team that he believes is going to win. That would be too easy. Instead, all bets are made on the basis of the expected difference in the final score.

Suppose Team A is figured to beat Team B by nine points. Nine points would be announced as the point spread, meaning that those who bet on Team A would collect only if Team A won by ten points or more.

Those who bet on Team B would collect only if Team B's final margin of loss was eight points or less.

If Team A won by nine points, the exact amount of the spread, nobody would win.

This means that when a gambler seeks to fix a basketball game, he doesn't have to get the players to "throw" the game, that is, to lose intentionally. All he has to do is entice the players on one team to reduce their scoring output, or, by defensive lapses, to permit the opposition to do more scoring than expected.

This system enables bookmakers to approach players with offers that seem to be only slightly dishonest. "What's the difference if you win by only six points instead of ten?" a fixer will say. "You're not really letting down the school or the team. You're not losing the game, just easing up a little."

Young men who fall for this line make a tragic mistake. Honesty does not come in degrees. A person can either be trusted or he cannot be. There is no middle ground. Shaving points is just as wrong, both morally and legally, as throwing a game.

What Henry Hill wanted the bribed Boston College players to do was rig things so that Boston College would win by less than the betting line when the team was favored. Or he wanted the team to lose by more than the line when it was rated the underdog. Hill and his associates would always bet on Boston College's opponent.

The first of the rigged games was against Harvard. It took place on December 16, 1978. Boston College was favored by twelve points. Hill bet fifteen thousand dollars on Harvard to lose by less than twelve. He was "just testing the water," he said.

Hill watched the game, sitting with Tony and Rocca Perla amidst the Boston College fans. What he saw made him feel great. He saw Sweeney throw the ball away three times. He saw Kuhn fumble the ball out of bounds. On another play, a Harvard player missed a free throw, grabbed the rebound, and drove around Kuhn and scored.

BOSTON COLLEGE HAS TO STRUGGLE PAST SCRAPPY HARVARD, declared a headline in a Boston paper the next day. The margin of victory was three points. "Everybody went home happy . . ." said Hill.

In the games that followed, Tony Perla was Hill's contact with the players. Through Perla, Hill would inform the players about the betting line on the game.

In some games, Kuhn and Sweeney were unable to rig the outcome as Hill instructed, even though they tried. They said they had to include Ernie Cobb in their scheme because Cobb was the key man on the Boston College team. Cobb, twenty-four years old, five-foot-eleven, from Stamford, Connecticut, was co-captain with Sweeney in 1978-79, averaging 21.3 points a game. "We've got to have Cobb," the players insisted.

Hill instructed Perla to have the other players talk to Cobb. Not long after, Hill received word that Cobb was enthusiastic, but that it was going to cost him an additional twenty-five hundred dollars a game as Cobb's contribution.

In the article he wrote in *Sports Illustrated*, Hill named nine games that were fixed. In addition to the Harvard game, the players rigged scores in games against U.C.L.A., Rhode Island, Holy Cross, Fordham, St. John's Holy Cross, and Connecticut twice, according to Hill.

All of this came to light after Hill joined the Federal Witness Program, becoming a government informer. Federal authorities questioned him about the huge robbery of cash and jewels from a cargo terminal at Kennedy Airport. Specifically, they wanted to know what Hill had done with himself in the days immediately following the robbery.

The robbery took place on December 11, 1978. On December 16, 1978, Boston College played Harvard, the first of the games fixed by Hill. In explaining why he happened to be attending the game, Hill disclosed the details of the betting scheme.

Late in 1981, Rick Kuhn was convicted by a federal court in Brooklyn of having taken part in the point-shaving scheme. He was later sentenced to ten years' imprisonment. That was believed to be the stiffest punishment ever given to a college athlete for fixing games.

Government investigators said at the time they were continuing to probe the role that had been played by Ernie Cobb in the conspiracy. Jim Sweeney was a key Government witness at Kuhn's trial.

The point-shaving scheme that involved Boston College was not the first time that college basketball had been tainted by a fixing scandal. Far from it.

Early in 1945, gamblers tried to have Brooklyn College lose to Akron in an attempted betting coup. But the gamblers failed. They tried again in January 1949, trying to get George Washington University to lose to Manhattan. But they failed again.

In January 1951, gamblers approached Junius Kellogg, a sophomore center for Manhattan College, and offered him one thousand dollars to make sure Manhattan lost to DePaul University by ten points or more.

Junius was shaken by the offer. Not only did he say no, he told his coach about it. The coach called in officials of the college who went to the police. Two bookmakers were arrested as a result.

The gamblers kept trying. Later in 1951 and in 1952 the lives of thirty-two boys were blighted when it was revealed that they had sold out to gamblers. The best college teams in the country and at least ten All-America nominees were implicated.

Three stars of the University of Kentucky team that was part of the United States squad in the 1948 Olympic games, a team that had won two consecutive N.C.A.A. (National Collegiate Athletic Association) championships took payments to fix games.

Seven players representing C.C.N.Y. (City College of New York), which had been dubbed basketball's "Cinderella Team" for the unprecedented feat of winning both the N.C.A.A. title and the N.I.T. (National Invitation Tournament), were found to have played ball with fixers. So did eight players from Bradley University, the runner-up to C.C.N.Y. in the N.C.A.A. tourney and the N.I.T.

Then there was the case of L.I.U. (Long Island University). In the 1951 season, L.I.U. was undefeated in sixteen games and seemed headed for the number one ranking in the polls. Then three key men on the team were accused of having taken eighteen thousand five hundred dollars in bribes and fixing, or attempting to fix, seven games over two seasons. With their names in the headlines almost daily, the players went to pieces, and L.I.U. lost four consecutive games that were strictly on the level. Later, five more L.I.U. players admitted to District Attorney Frank S. Hogan of New York that they had worked with gamblers. Hogan's investigations also involved Manhattan College, N.Y.U. (New York University), and the University of Toledo.

The fixed games were first revealed because of the suspicions of Max Kase, sports editor of *The New York Journal-American*. For months, Kase believed that gamblers had a hand in the outcome of games at Madison Square Garden. He began dropping in to spots where gamblers met. He asked questions and listened. He also turned *Journal-American* reporters loose on the job of trying to pin down the "fix guy" who was arranging the player bribes.

One night a "source" gave Kase a name, the final piece in the puzzle. Kase took the information he had gathered to the district attorney. Not long after, the *Journal-American* announced the arrest of L.I.U. and C.C.N.Y. players.

Also arrested was the money man, one Salvatore Sollazzo, a New York gambler, jewelry manufacturer, and ex-convict. Late in 1951, Sollazzo was sentenced to a prison term of from eight to sixteen years.

Exactly ten years later, in 1961, it happened again. This time thirty-seven more players were named, twenty-two more colleges, and forty-four more games. The dumpers and the gamblers who bribed them were uncovered by the New York District Attorney's office and North Carolina State Bureau of Investigation. There were more fix exposures in 1965.

One question that is always asked is why didn't the coach or other players suspect that a particular game was fixed. Don't the "honest" players see things on the court that can lead them to believe something funny is going on?

The answer is no. When the point spread is big enough— eight or up to twelve points, say — two or three players can control the number of points scored without any danger of being detected by their coach or teammates. In fact, a group of really skilled practitioners can win the game for their team and still make the score come out the way the gamblers want it. They can even end up as stars of the game, and see themselves hailed in the newspaper accounts of the contest the next day.

Let's take a close look at a game that was known to be fixed, in which Bradley University defeated Oregon State. Two days before the game,

Gene Melchiorre, Bradley's All-America guard met the pay-off man for a group of New York gamblers in the lobby of a Chicago hotel, and was handed an envelope containing four thousand dollars.

The four thousand-dollar bribe was paid to Melchiorre for the role he played in "shaving" heavily favored Bradley's margin of victory over the Oregon team. The spread for the game was ten points. The gamblers put their money on Oregon State — not to win — but to "beat" the spread, that is, to lose by less than the quoted ten-point margin. Since Bradley had won by only three points, the gamblers prospered. Melchiorre pocketed two thousand dollars of the bribe money and admitted to distributing the remainder among some of his teammates.

The day after the game, headlines in the *Peoria Star*, Bradley's hometown newspaper, declared: BRADLEY TURNS BACK OREGON STATE, 77-74; SQUEAK, FRED COUNT 21 APIECE.

"Squeak," or "Squeaky," was Melchiorre; Fred was Fred Schlictman, one of the three Bradley players who admitted to dividing the four thousand dollars with Melchiorre (although he denied knowing of the fix in advance). According to officials, Schlictman received five hundred dollars, Aaron Preece, one thousand dollars, and Jim Kelly, five hundred dollars.

The newspaper's account of the game hailed Melchiorre and Schlictman for leading the Bradley attack. And why not. Between them Melchiorre and Schlictman scored forty-two points, more than half of Bradley's total.

Later, coach Forddy Anderson of Bradley commented on the contest. "I've studied the movies of the Oregon State game at least twenty times," he said, "and I can't find a single play which indicates the kids weren't giving their best efforts every second."

Hank Fisher, who had been broadcasting play-by-play accounts of Bradley games over a Peoria radio station for several years, had this to say: "In a stretch of more than one hundred games, I hardly took my eyes off the ball, and in all that time I never saw a movement by a Bradley player — against Oregon State or any other opponent — which looked suspicious."

One of the players involved in the scandal explained his method of point shaving. "You simply played your hardest on defense," he said. "Nobody pays much attention to defense. So you let the man you're supposed to guard get half a step ahead of you. He breaks loose and scores but who can say you didn't try to stop him."

Of course, coaches can and do stop defensive mistakes. But a coach would have to be a mind reader to be able to tell when a player's mistake was deliberate.

When L.I.U. coach Clair Bee was asked why he never suspected games were fixed, he replied, "I never dreamed a boy who played for me could be crooked. Had I thought it necessary to police his conduct off the court, I would have given up coaching."

Even when Bee watched filmed replays of fixed games, he couldn't spot any actions that he might question. "I studied the movies a hundred times," he said, "and I can point out where the bribed boys played more spectacularly in fixes than they did when they were leveling."

Some years ago, Yale basketball coach Howard Hobson was conducting a basketball clinic in Boston. "What is the one basic requirement for a winning team?" asked one of the coaches attending the clinic.

"Shooting. You need good shooters," Hobson answered. "The idea of the game is to get the ball in the basket."

Another coach disagreed. "Passing," he said. "A good team may use three hundred to three hundred fifty passes in a game. It's basic to everything else."

A third voice was heard from the balcony. "You're both wrong," this coach said. "Material is the basic requirement for winning games."

Most coaches agree. If you have the material, that is, if you have highly skilled, highly motivated players, you'll have shooters and passers, and you'll win games.

Bringing in material involves recruiting. "Look," says one coach. "I've got to win. I'm in a tough league. The other schools are beating the bushes for players. I've got to recruit right along with them or I'll be in the cellar in the standings. I don't have any choice."

The problem of basketball's betting scandals is rooted in recruiting. Standard recruiting practices involve giving the athlete a scholarship or, as it's often called, a "free ride." This includes tuition, room and board, book fees, lab fees, and the like.

There's nothing wrong with giving someone an athletic scholarship. Doing so gives an individual who otherwise might not have been able to obtain a college education an opportunity to improve himself by taking advantage of his athletic ability.

What has happened, however, is that some colleges go beyond the legal free ride. Aid given athletes has taken the form of new cars, bank accounts, cash payments, and regular monthly salaries for jobs supervised by the athletic department. In some cases, athletes have received cash from university officials through the overpayment of expenses or by giving the athletes extra tickets to "sold out" games, tickets which they would sell.

In New York City, a judge trying a fixing case disclosed that one player received a job in addition to tuition, room, meals, and books. He was told he would not have to put in any time at the job. Whenever he gave a good athletic performance, his pay slip would be marked "extra hours," and he would receive an additional sum of money.

Once a young player begins taking illegal payments for playing basketball, how big a step is it before he starts taking illegal payments for shaving points?

Newspapers across the country also have to shoulder some of the blame. Much of the gambling on basketball, and all of the bribe cases, developed after the press began to publicize the point spread. Today, most daily newspapers continue to feature the betting odds in their pre-game stories.

Another factor is the "win-at-any-cost" climate in which the game is played. Alumni groups demand winning teams. If a coach fails to win, he's fired.

Of course, the players themselves have to bear the ultimate responsibility. There would never be a fix if a player didn't say yes to a fixer.

Why do players do it?

Ray Paprocky of N.Y.U. cooperated with fixers because he was married, and his wife was expecting their first child, his father had just died, he commuted three hours a day to and from school, and he worked an eight-hour shift in a fruit-canning plant. "I'm aware what I did was wrong," Paprocky said in an article that appeared in *Sport* magazine. "But if I were in the same circumstances, I'd do it again, not because I want to, but because I was forced to. It was better than robbing a grocery store."

What about Sherman White, the L.I.U. star who sacrificed a glittering career as a professional star? Why did he do it? "Come on in," a friend said to White. "It's a great chance to make some money. You want good clothes, don't you? You've got a girl and you want to marry her. Don't be a sucker. Everybody else is making money out of the thing. Why don't you?"

Fred Portnoy, who participated in the fixing

of games at Columbia, said this: "You know it is morally wrong, but you don't think it is criminally wrong. You know you never would have done it if there had been a threat of jail. Another thing: I didn't have much loyalty to Columbia. I knew we didn't have a good team, so if we lost by five points or ten points what was the difference?"

Why did Boston College's Jim Sweeney do it? "The money, man, the money," said Henry Hill. "That's why we all did it."

In July 1980, the Organized Crime Strike Force for the Eastern District of New York began investigating the fixed basketball games involving Boston College. Evidence was later presented to a federal grand jury. Both Ernie Cobb and Jim Sweeney were believed to be cooperating with federal investigators.

In the final analysis, the hows and whys of the various fixed games don't mean much. The results are always the same. Fine young men with promise, with every chance for professional and personal success, have their lives wrecked.